S0-BIG-498

Caro Riccardo,
        Sempre avanti!
                Stefano

1/30/19

Maybe-Ism

THE EMOJI BRAIN IN SEARCH OF A PERSONAL GOD

Stephen L. DeFelice, M.D.

authorHOUSE®

AuthorHouse™
1663 Liberty Drive
Bloomington, IN 47403
www.authorhouse.com
Phone: 1 (800) 839-8640

© 2018 Stephen L. DeFelice, M.D. All rights reserved.

No part of this book may be reproduced, stored in a retrieval system, or transmitted by any means without the written permission of the author.

Published by AuthorHouse 07/20/2018

ISBN: 978-1-5462-5296-2 (sc)
ISBN: 978-1-5462-5295-5 (hc)
ISBN: 978-1-5462-5294-8 (e)

Library of Congress Control Number: 2018907991

Print information available on the last page.

Any people depicted in stock imagery provided by Getty Images are models, and such images are being used for illustrative purposes only. Certain stock imagery © Getty Images.

This book is printed on acid-free paper.

Because of the dynamic nature of the Internet, any web addresses or links contained in this book may have changed since publication and may no longer be valid. The views expressed in this work are solely those of the author and do not necessarily reflect the views of the publisher, and the publisher hereby disclaims any responsibility for them.

The DeFelice Library

Non-fiction

Drug Discovery: The Pending Crisis, 1972
From Oysters to Insulin: Nature and Medicine at Odds, 1986
Memory Loss: Normal vs. Abnormal, 1988
Nutraceuticals: Developing, Claiming and Marketing Medical Foods, 1998
The Carnitine Defense, 1999
The Attack on the White Male – And the Weakening of America, 2010
Maybe-Ism: The Emoji Brain in Search of a Personal God, 2018

Fiction

Old Italian Neighborhood Values, 2002
He Made Them Young Again, 2006
The Man Who Made Love to More Women than Casanova and the Apocalyptic Aphrodisiac, 2013
Dr. Julian: What Woman Do You Want Me to Be? A Doctor's Gender Sexploration with Three Women, 2017

Biography

A Maverick's Odyssey, One Doctor's Quest to Conquer Disease by Michael Mannion, 2007

To Friendship

Aristotle and Francis Bacon wrote beautifully about friendship and how it wears many faces. Also, there's an old saying that, "A friend in need is a friend indeed." And I am truly a lucky a man to have two such friends who, in different ways, not only encouraged me but actually involved themselves in the creation of this book.

First to Patricia Park my indispensable colleague of many more moons than she—or I!—would like to admit, for her tenacious nonstop energy and exceptional creativity not only in critiquing what I wrote but adding invaluable suggestions to expand and clarify its content.

Second to Michael Mannion, a gifted and now senior author as well as founder of the Mindshift Institute, whose literary wisdom and know-how opened a number of important doors.

A special note of appreciation to the talented artist, Dyer Wilk, for his creative adaptation and modification of Michelangelo's Sistine Chapel masterpiece on the cover and the Chapter 7 illustration, Raphael's School of Athens.

Contents

Chapter 1

MAYBE-ISM

Miguel Unamuno boldly declared, "What use is there for God, if there is no immortality?"

I agree.

Many have declared that it's impossible to prove the definite existence of God, let alone a personal one. Many have also declared that it is impossible to disprove his existence.

I also agree.

In order to believe in and communicate with a personal god, one must have faith.

Once more, I agree. And for the record, I once had and embraced such faith, but it somehow abandoned me.

So why then did I write this book?

It's due to the undeniable, growing and persuasive, but not definitive, weight of evidence that supports Maybe-Ism.

And what, you may ask, is Maybe-Ism?

Generally speaking, arguments regarding the existence of a personal god as the creator of mankind can be divided into three categories: Godism, which supports the existence of such a God; agnosticism which maintains that we can never know of his existence though it certainly may be possible, and atheism, which outright rejects his existence in any form. Maybe-Ism is a new "ism" category that falls between Godism and traditional agnosticism but sits much closer to the former.

There is little doubt that the decline of belief in God, let alone a personal one, has accelerated over the past half-century energetically spearheaded by intellectual and influential secular thought leaders who continue to dominate the attack against God's existence. Tradition and religious beliefs are fast fading with weakening and surprisingly ineffectual opposition against the anti-God forces. The causes are many but can largely be attributed to technology and secularism driven Scientism—the belief that science and reason can explain all.

But there is one principal reason why the Godism advocates are ineffectual which first dawned on me during the late 70s when I owned and managed a company that planned and placed clinical studies on new medical therapies at various university medical institutions. I was looking for someone to take my place as manager when I thought of a highly promising medical doctor whom I knew with lots of clinical research experience. He was young, highly intelligent, creative and well-met with a positive outlook on life. In addition, he was a good guy, and I liked the man.

We met at a small, delightful family-owned Italian restaurant in Greenwich Village just across the street from the former St. Vincent's Medical Center. Things were going well until I made the job offer. His facial demeanor turned suddenly sullen, and he remained uncomfortably silent. I decided to break the ice and asked him if anything was wrong. He took a deep breath and replied, "Doctor DeFelice, though I'm thrilled with the offer, I can't accept it. You see, I have AIDS."

He was the son of an Italian-American Catholic and a German-born Jewish mother neither of whom was particularly religious. Over the years he gradually lost his interest in whatever modicum of belief that he had in God. When he found out that he had AIDS, he naturally began to contemplate whether there is a God and afterlife. Who wouldn't? At that time and place it wasn't appropriate to pursue this subject. We, instead, discussed potential promising therapies in the AIDS research pipeline. Unfortunately, there were few.

Well I decided to stay in periodic contact with him as his clinical condition went inexorably downhill. During his final days, he called me regarding my opinion of a recent anti-viral therapy with anti-AIDS potential. His voice was weak and for some reason I raised the subject of his current religious beliefs and his thoughts of a possible afterlife. He, with newfound vocal strength, angrily shot back, "I'm still an atheist; I'm a goddam confirmed atheist." In order to maintain some level of hope, I very diplomatically suggested that he should not close the book on this subject for there were billions of people around the world who did have faith in a God, and this reality must be respected and looked into.

Now I appreciated his straightforwardness regarding his atheism but was puzzled by the volcanic anger behind it. Something had changed and I asked him why and his response first opened my eyes to what was going on and which I continued to sadly observe up until today. He did take my advice and researched the major arguments for the pros and cons of not only the existence of a personal god but also the possibility that he would meet his departed mom and dad after his final hour.

The results of his research were as follows: there was no scientific or credible objective evidence for the existence of God let alone an afterlife. He said that supporting arguments were based on emotional, non-quantifiable testimonials such as the Bible and wordy philosophical-theological theories. He needed, however, some concrete, objective and other substantial measurable data or arguments to convince him to even begin to consider such possibilities.

I did visit with him one more time during which he, his mind was still sharp as can be, caught me off guard and asked, "Steve, I forgot to ask you whether you believed in a personal god and afterlife. Do you?" I, without hesitation, answered, "Steve," we both had the same first name, "Maybe." And then we slowly shook hands both sensing that we'd never meet again.

Since then times have radically changed! Paradoxically, the growing weight of evidence of Scientism combined with the Emoji-sensitive nature of the brain along with other objective-type evidence such as human signaling persuasively support Maybe-Ism far outweighing the claims of evidence-based atheism which ignores such evidence. And this book will try to make that case.

Who should read this book? I did not write it to proselytize the unbelievers to convert to Godism but, instead, to those who already have faith to various degrees and how Maybe-Ism can strengthen such faith. And, just as importantly, to arm the influential leaders of faith, including the laity, with such solid evidence to, with justified confidence, counter the apparently inexorable onslaught of secular Scientism.

...

I was born on April 14th, 1936, the day President Lincoln was shot and the Titanic sank. Also, during my college days, for some reason, I was curious regarding the month of the birth of Jesus Christ. I don't remember how I came to the conclusion that it happened sometime in mid-April. Excited by this finding and being an egoistic optimist by nature, I concluded it must have been on April 14th!

During the period spanning from 1936 to 2018, four generations, I came to observe the most radical, exploding and unsettling, destabilizing change in human history, which acceleration, fueled by increasing intrusive technology, continues unabated.

Now put yourself in my place. I, a first generation Italian, was born in Philadelphia in a neighborhood of largely Italian immigrants. There were no televisions or phones. We did, however, have a radio in our home. Every week day night with eager anticipation and while lying on the floor, I listened to a number of thirty-minute adventure episodes, my favorite one being the Lone Ranger which was accompanied by Rossini's energetic operatic William Tell Overture score. Then arrived the beginning of the technology explosion in our home. During the late 40s or thereabouts, a television and phone entered through our doors. There were only three television channels, and the phone was a party-line one shared by one or more other homes.

Around the age of 12, something happened that profoundly changed my life. My father and mentor began to teach me about philosophy and the lives of philosophers. For some reason, he seemed to favor the Stoics. One of the first stories that I'll never forget dealt with the Greek slave Stoic, Epictetus. While his master was twisting his arm, he warned him that if he continued to do so, his arm would break. The master ignored his warning and continued to do the twisting until Epictetus's arm broke, after which the slave "stoically" commented, "Master, I told you so." Anyway, after hearing and reading about the other Stoics such as Marcus Aurelius and Seneca, I decided that I didn't want to become a Stoic—not at all!

It was that giant intellect, Aristotle, who sent me on a disciplined path which has guided much of my life. It was his three-word advice about life—"Observe, observe, observe." And there have been highly curious observers throughout the ages. *An Apology for Idlers* is one of my favorite teaching short stories written by Robert Louis Stevenson, the author of *Dr. Jekyll and Mr. Hyde.* It's about a boy caught playing hooky from school by an elderly man who scolds him for avoiding the lessons being taught in the classroom. The entire dialogue deals with the truant student who, with razor-sharp reasoning, defends the importance of being idle and alone because it released his brain's curiosity to more easily observe, observe and observe in order to think about life on his own.

Centuries before Stevenson, Leonardo Da Vinci gave a *saper veder* (knowing how to see) advice to young painters when they walked through the fields observing various objects. "As you go through the fields, turn your attention to various objects, and, in turn look now at this thing and now at that, collecting a store of diverse facts… Do not do as some painters who… though they see the objects, do not comprehend them."

Aristotle would certainly have applauded the advice of these two diverse personalities.

Returning to my old neighborhood: what I observed after World War II was the unifying nationalistic spirit of the times characterized by vibrant patriotism, optimism, the embrace of traditional values such as religion, marriage and importance of the family. Divorce was rare and almost everyone had a job. Atheism and agnosticism were rarely mentioned, let alone discussed. The existence of a personal god was a given, and the organized religions of Christianity were still going strong, or at least were not yet surrendering to the inexorable forces of technology.

With the passing of time what I then observed was that things, continually driven by advancing technology, began to dramatically accelerate, and God, along with our post-war, cultural-binding values, began to fade from center stage of our country.

Let's now turn to my personal rendezvous with faith in a personal god: For certain reasons, I never went to a Catholic school whereas many of my childhood friends attended the neighborhood one where they learned about Catholicism and its beliefs and rituals. Though I was baptized and received the other sacraments of Holy Communion and Confirmation, I did not appreciate the rationale behind them and other Catholic teachings.

Now I'd like to tell you about my confounding, yet mystically enlightening encounter with faith. Now don't ask me why I fully experienced and embraced it because I don't have a definitive answer. I was always curious to learn more about the Catholic religion, and when I was in my third year of college I decided to find out. Little did I know that I was off to a beautiful adventure with God which somehow regrettably and slowly expired by the end of my second year in medical school, four years later.

While a student at Temple University, I took a few night and summer classes related to philosophy and theology at Saint Joseph's, a Jesuit college, and Villanova, an Augustinian one. What initially surprised me was how the Catholic Church heavily employs the use of reason in matters related to God, himself, in addition to the elevated mystical and ritual aspects of its religious teachings. I, being genetically curious, was very much impressed and encouraged by what I read and heard.

But even after this effort and being taught by some superb philosophy and theology professors and heavily pondering about the rationale or reasoning arguments of the Catholic, and, yes, non-Catholic religious literature, I was not only very much discouraged but outright frustrated. Despite absorbing the collective wisdom of much that I encountered, it did not bring me any closer to a personal god which I was seeking. Sure, I understood and appreciated the intellectual and religious points of view, but I really became discouraged for it did not give me the faith that I was searching for—the powerful convincing belief, not based on science or conscious reasoning, to believe and communicate with and be close to him. It reminds me of the computer world where there is contact without personal contact. I want to make it clear that my search was directed to God, himself, and not at any particular religion though I certainly concentrated on Catholicism.

Then I decided to concentrate on the works of the mystics and other deeply religious believers, mostly Catholic, such as St. Francis of Assisi and Teresa di Avila, who were overwhelmingly in love with a personal god without employing the use of reason. In other words, they had the thing called faith where reason can't take you. What was common were two things— praying to and having a conversation with God, which you may think are the same thing, but they are not, not at all! You'll have to try it to find out.

Then it happened— and, for the life of me, I cannot explain why. While I began to pray and talk to God daily, faith gradually arrived in full force. I had finally made personal contact! I became unbudgeably convinced that there is a personal god and, to boot, also a personal afterlife. It's difficult to put into words how it played out, but I'll give it a try.

Let's start with some details. The Catholic Church teaches that there are three persons in a single God— the Father, Son or Jesus and the Holy Spirit whose mystical union is called the Trinity and which belief, may I add, is supported by the New Testament. It's a complicated story but, in real life, the believers either pray directly to God or Jesus as a single entity believing that they are both the same with respect to receiving and responding to one's message or request. I never, however, met anyone who prayed to the Holy Spirit. I communicated to either God or Jesus, but I, on each occasion, hadn't the slightest idea why I chose to pray or talk to one and not the other. Many Catholics also pray to Mary, the mother of Jesus, to ask for her help to get their messages across to her son. Don't get cynical for there is a beauty in this belief. It helps lots of people with their faith, and we all agree that we need all the help we can get in life! It's interesting to note, that in the Quran, Mary is the only woman mentioned by name.

While I prayed and talked to God every day, I continued to read heavily about Catholicism and other religions, including those of the Reformation, which added to the depth of my belief and understanding how people relate to God. I attended the Catholic Mass as often as I could much preferring the quietness of the way Mass was in those days to the noisy ones of today which, in my opinion, detract one from going to a higher spiritual level of communication with God.

How did I feel during my rendezvous with God? There was no religious high; no swoons or rushes of adrenalin which, to tell the truth, I would have welcomed with open arms - and still do. I can't say that I was happy for I'm not sure what happiness is but, after awakening each morning, I almost always looked forward to the day. I just felt calm, confident and strong on a higher level than previously. It reinforced what my mother and father had already taught me and permanently stamped it in my mind about life's values such as don't think of yourself too much, help others as much as reasonable, particularly your family, don't think about material things too much, keep your word and be strong and independent. These qualities, without doubt, are effective personal characteristics extremely helpful in order to accommodate to life's constant problems. And technology is rapidly making life increasingly complex and difficult.

After classes, I worked at various jobs; and at night, after I finished my studies, I would usually take myself to selected favorite local bars to enjoy a couple of beers and observe the body language of the customers while listening to them talk about a variety of subjects ranging from their personal problems to who would be the next heavyweight boxing champion of the world. I did some of my best writing there and still occasionally do but, regrettably, at my age my journeys there are few and far between. To repeat, sitting on a bar stool, observing and listening to others, is a great learning experience. It's like being with a superb teacher. One of my secret desires, which I hid from mom and dad, was to be a part-time bartender and learn, first hand, what goes on in the minds of all types of people. The right dose of alcohol is like a priest in the confessional booth of the Catholic Church. It helps loosen the tongue and oftentimes makes a temporary honest person. Harvard's Law School club motto, *In Vino Veritas,* or wine makes one speak the truth, was embraced by Benjamin Franklin.

Now here's the unexplainable, puzzling and frustrating mystery that happened while I was in medical school. My relationship and faith in God slowly faded away. It did not happen overnight because of some unfathomable personal tragedy: God simply left my life and, regrettably, he has yet to return.

During the late 60s I was, as a physician consultant, called upon to treat a highly intelligent patient with miliary or widespread tuberculosis who taught me a lesson that I never forgot. He asked, "Doctor DeFelice, who knows more about tuberculosis, you or me?" I, not quite sure why he asked the question, replied, "Honestly, I'm not sure. Why do you ask?"

"Well, who knows more about my disease; you, the doctor who knows the facts about it and is treating me, or me, the patient, who has the disease and is experiencing it?"

Momentarily stumped, I asked, "Mr. Morgan"—I shall never forget his name—"who do you think knows more?"

His tired eyes suddenly exuded a spark of momentary energy, and he replied, "The patient, of course: no question about it, Doctor DeFelice. I know more about my disease than you do." This provocative interchange got me thinking for a long time. It then dawned on me that there are three categories of people who deal with the existence of faith and a personal god: Those who have the faith, those who had and then lost it and those – be they agnostic or atheist - who never did. According to Mr. Morgan, and I agree, the latter are at a profound disadvantage when objectively dealing with addressing the existence of a potential personal god simply because they never have experienced it. So keep this in mind.

And, before I go on, it is fair to know what my current position is regarding a personal god. I've now converted from an agnostic to a Maybe-Ist. It's akin to what the wondering philosopher, Santayana, allegedly replied to one of his students when asked about his belief on the existence of God. He replied, "There is no God, but Mary is his mother!"

The approach of this book is broad-based ranging from the human brain to transcendental mindsets of cultures to the universe and evolution, among others. Of unique and special note is the discussion of the Emoji Brain interpreting much of reality as icons or symbols. This points out that there is, coupled with objective data and numbers such as discussed in the Human Signaler section, a superior level of what humans can know that supersedes ordinary methods of thought including that employed by theologians, philosophers and scientists.

The branch of philosophy which deals with how and what we can know is called epistemology. It is not an exciting branch but essential to grasp and understand before proceeding on to the evidence supporting Maybe-Ism.

So persevere, and let's start off by tackling the critical, difficult subject of epistemology.

Chapter 2

EPISTEMOLOGY AND
THE EMOJI BRAIN

For anyone in modern times who is interested in discussing or promoting the idea of whether a God exists, it's mandatory to be sufficiently versed in epistemology, that branch of philosophy which deals with how and what you or I or anyone else can know: what is true, not true and not knowable and how we can make that judgement. Any thoughts, opinions and interpretation of events, including those of science, are subject to some form of epistemological interpretation. Unfortunately, it is one of the most boring and complicated fields in philosophy which has been, and continues to be, as with video games, dominated almost exclusively by men. *Unlike the playing of games, however, the difference, which is critical for you to grasp, is that with every epistemological system, there are no winners!* One philosopher proposes and the other easily disposes. Epistemology is unlike the physical sciences where experimentation and mathematical research are objectively quantified by the use of number: $2+2=4$ and $E=mc^2$, and that's that. There's no doubt about it. If, however, a student who majors in philosophy and matriculates for four years at a reputable university, religious or secular, is asked what he or she can know, they will either be understandably confused or embrace a faulty system simply because, to repeat, all systems are faulty. Few are aware that a mediocre logician can destroy any epistemological argument but another mediocre logician can dismember his argument. The deeper one probes the deeper one sinks.

Does quicksand jump to mind? Those men who continually try to come up with a valid epistemological system must suffer from some form of tenacious and enjoyable masochism. Many of the great philosophers such as Francis Bacon and Nietzsche largely avoided dealing with it. They, fortunately for their peace of mind, had other things to do.

There are many ways of attempts at knowing such as the use of reason and the scientific method, intuition, common sense and a host of others. Now, you may ask, what's the problem? Why the dilemma? Why, after centuries of debates, do we continue to fail to come up with a generally acceptable epistemological system particularly when it comes to subject matter that's virtually non-quantifiable such as the existence of a transcendent being or personal god? The answer, you will be surprised to learn, is clear and not too difficult to grasp. *It's primarily the elaborate use and interpretation of words—YES, WORDS!—in the written and verbal language of expression.*

Though I found it hard to believe in our cyberspace era, Science magazine reported that in today's world of disappearing languages, there are still approximately 7,000 remaining living ones—2,562 in Africa; 2,762 in Asia and the Pacific; 396 in Europe and 1,132 in the Americas. Depending on how they are counted, the English language has approximately 200,000 words and Spanish has 100,000 ones; so let's take 150,000 as the average of all languages and multiply it by 7,000 which amounts to a lot of words! But there's more than numbers involved, for many words have different connotations in different languages, which colors the meaning of the use of such words.

Another critical point: It's generally way underappreciated that the origin and purpose of words was primarily due to the need to communicate with others and not to precisely define things. "Hey, Joe, watch out! There's a hungry dinosaur on the other side of the mountain so watch your back side" and not, "Joe, did you know that a dinosaur has twenty upper teeth and nineteen lower ones", etc. But, paradoxically, philosophers, theologians and everybody else continue to stubbornly heavily employ the use of words to define things— the very tool which is used to destroy their word-based arguments, explanations and beliefs. In addition to those aforementioned insurmountable epistemological barriers, there is yet an additional one. It involves the perception of the words by the user versus that of the receiver.

For example, just try asking people, which I often do, the six-worded question "What is the meaning of life?" and the brain, usually within less than thirty seconds, searches its memory bank of life's entire analyzed experiences and, please take careful note, responds either using a few words to a few sentences such as:

"Life is meaningless." Ecclesiastes of the Old Testament.

"You are born, you suffer and you die." Joseph Conrad, famous author of the past.

"You fall out of your mother's womb; you crawl across open country under fire, and drop into your grave." Quentin Crisp, famous curmudgeon of the past.

"Love life, above everything in the world…love it, regardless of logic as you say, it must be regardless of logic, and it's only then one will understand the meaning of it." Fyodor Dostoevsky, historic Russian novelist.

"We must free ourselves to be loved by God." Saint Teresa, a beloved Catholic nun.

"Life on earth is only a preparation for the eternal home, which is far more important than the short pleasures that seduce us here." Muhammad Ali, former great heavyweight champion of the world.

Since we are dealing with unquestionable intellectual quicksand without the clarity of objective quantification, why does my recommendation urging you to understand epistemology by the use of words, make any sense? One has no choice simply because for all arguments supporting the existence or non-existence of God are largely based on some form of epistemology be it by reason or mysticism or some other mechanism. In today's world where secular intellectuals, particularly those in our universities supported by the media are dominating the public arena using faulty, elaborate wordy epistemological arguments influencing and misleading huge segments of our culture, you must have a general understanding of what they are talking about and how to respond. But, you may also legitimately ask, whether it's a futile, dead-end effort against such odds because it's too late to have an impact. *I, however,—hold on to your hats!—believe that there is a unique epistemological system which lends substantial persuasive credibility to the potential existence of God or Maybe-Ism.* So let's first begin by taking a quick look at these historic systems beginning in ancient Greece with the great historic duo, Plato and his student, Aristotle. This is not a critique of these or other systems but just to familiarize you with their existence and broad variety along with some brief notations.

Plato believed that we can never truly know what anything really is but only their shadows or vague images. For example, there are all kinds of trees in our world but we can't know what a universal or pure tree is for the simple reason it doesn't exist. But, he argues, it must exist somewhere and that somewhere is in the World of Ideas, but we have no idea where that world is. Aristotle, however, disagreed with his teacher and maintained that the concept of the universal tree is in the individual mind after it observes many trees in life, stores and analyzes the images in the brain and deduces the commonality among all of them—roots, trunks, branches and leaves.

Aristotle is recognized as the father of logic and particularly, though there were hints of it in the logic-less Hindu literature, for his creation of the syllogism, a critical tool in the use of reason. An example of the syllogism is as follows:

Humans are rational
Herman is a human
Therefore Herman is rational

Makes sense? Not so to many philosophers because his primary assumption, they argue, may not be universally true. For example, chimpanzees can behave rationally, so Herman could be a chimpanzee! Don't laugh. This is serious stuff in philosophical circles!

Aristotle's common sense general epistemological system was effectively endorsed by the great Catholic theologian, Thomas Aquinas, during the thirteenth century which system then dominated philosophical and theological circles until the seventeenth century upon the arrival of the brilliant revolutionary mathematician and Catholic philosopher, Descartes. He proposed to cast aside the rules of formal Aristotelean logic and begin with a system of universal doubt; in other words, start out by assuming that we know nothing. The first necessary step, of course, is to confirm his own existence in order to make his argument. After all, he must first exist in order to propose anything. Thus his famous proclamation, *Cogito ergo sum* or *I think therefore I am*, was that first epistemological step upon which he built his philosophical system. Now his Jesuits colleagues, who were his close friends, pointed out that by beginning with "I think" which contains the "I" word, he had already assumed his existence and the thinking part of his declaration is, therefore, irrelevant and the basis of his system falls flat.

Let's now jump to the eighteenth century to another revolutionary giant of philosophy, the atheistic skeptic, David Hume, who challenged—what else?— Aristotle's and Descartes's systems with another complicated one of extremely wordy systemic thought which still stubbornly resonates in Western philosophical circles. He, for example, denies that we can know much regarding the connection between cause and effect which we'll address later on. Then one day he declared, "Certitude is for fools" where even an average student would deduce that he logically cast doubts on his own system! This extraordinary brilliant man was so heavily steeped in epistemological quicksand that, one day while playing billiards with a friend, he panicked because he, at that point, doubted his own existence pleading with him to convince himself that he did indeed exist.

Now we come to another revolutionary giant of philosophy, Immanuel Kant, who was a very religious Christian. His epistemological system is ponderous and complicated. He, somewhat echoing Plato, believed that we cannot know what a thing-in-itself *(das Ding an sich)* really is but only its appearance. Regarding the biblical God, he was alarmed and taken aback by Hume's philosophy of skepticism which had been widely embraced by others to effectively promote atheism. He, contrary to Hume's belief that we can only know things through the input of our senses, claimed that we are, *a priori*, all born with certain types of transcendental knowledge already in the mind such as his "categorical imperative" which is fundamentally a form of the Golden Rule and which rule, by the way, in addition to the Bible, is found in many different cultures.

Let's skip through the other great philosophers and move on to the more relatively recent highly influential ones such as Hegel, Heidegger and the existentialists such as Sartre all of whom tackled epistemology and, not surprisingly, disagreed not only with each other but also with the other giants of the past. And, not surprisingly, all of their epistemological systems could not survive critical scrutiny by others.

The almost obsessive elaborate use of reason, dramatically influenced by the explosion of the use of the scientific method and increased scientific discovery, was further embraced by the leaders of the secular intellectual communities and still continues on this torturous path. Post-modernism, analytic philosophy and its extension, deconstructionism, are three major resultant systems. The core tenant of post-modernism is based on the assumption that there are no absolute truths, including the objective existence of moral values, echoing the famous declaration by the Greek Sophist philosopher, Protagoras, that, "Man is the measure of all things." Everything is relative so, there's nothing wrong with telling lies or eliminating your enemy if you can get away with it. Stalin, though not fully appreciated by postmodernists, was a bona fide apostolic postmodernist in action. When asked how he would deal with an enemy, he said he would just simply, *alla* Machiavelli, eliminate him. He kept by his bedside a copy of Machiavelli's, *The Prince*. Analytic linguistic philosophy advocates such as Bertrand Russell, and Ludwig Wittgenstein unsuccessfully deal with the technical analysis of language and concepts, occasionally employing mathematical approaches.

Deconstructionism is a natural extension of the analytical approach. Its major advocate was the late Jacques Derrida. An example to where the intensive search for meaning of word-based language inevitably leads us was, frankly speaking, presented to me by a friend. Just as someone was about to enter a hotel elevator, he noticed a poster on the side saying, "Only seeing-eye dogs are permitted." A deconstructionist would interpret it as a warning that humans were not permitted to enter the elevator, let alone with their baggage as well as non-seeing eye dogs or anyone or anything else! Imagine employing this type of reasoning in every aspect of life where words are used the meaning of which is not clear and can be interpreted in multiple ways. It would drive one to insanity before the first sunset!

Though these epistemological systems, like others, do offer some insight into what we can, as human beings, know about life, all fail the ultimate test of overcoming the limitations of reason with the elaborate use of words. They are all unequivocally faulty.

So where does that lead us when it is generally accepted that there is no credible solution regarding the search of what we can know with justifiable certitude? The answer is to find a new epistemological system that makes more sense. And that system exists in those three pounds of flesh, the Emoji Brain.

THE EMOJI BRAIN

What I call the Emoji Brain is the part of the epistemological system on which human beings most commonly rely to encounter and deal with reality. It's critical to understand its role particularly when searching for the potential existence of a transcendental being such as a personal god. It takes us to where reason, the elaborate use of words and science, including mathematics, cannot go—not even close! For puzzling reasons this unequivocal fact has escaped sufficient recognition by leading religious advocates. As most of you know, an Emoji is a small, symbolic digital icon, usually a face, increasingly used in electronic messages and websites that represents and effectively summarizes an entity such as thoughts, feelings, opinions and other subject matter. It frequently is not a standalone icon but included or attached to a worded message to augment the impact of such message.

It's also critical to understand that the human brain is not an Emoji one, itself, but it, under many circumstances, interprets the world which it encounters and perceives as Emoji icons or symbols. This ability enormously increases its capacity to understand and cope with reality. It is essential for survival.

The brain operates on two levels— input and output. Input largely comes through the senses and internal forces where it receives, stores and analyzes what is fed to it. In addition, it has the capacity to remember and recall much of the stored information. Its input begins with the fetus in the environment of the mother's womb to one's final hour. Over the course of a day, let alone a lifetime as we shall see, there are trillions upon trillions of physical and mental inputs, yes-trillions!, such as biological signals, thoughts, feelings, routine daily chores at home or at work, encounters with others either experienced consciously or unconsciously. There are those who can remember the details of each day over a fifty-year period offering a trove of information for researchers.

With each passing day, the enormous quantity of human experiences are not only stored in the brain but in some mysterious way they, like an inverted pyramid, not only accumulate as separate experiences but become connected. Thus, if you experience one thing, another jumps to mind. This interconnectivity phenomenon can take one to higher levels of feeling and thought than that which has actually been experienced. For example, the death of a loved one can take the brain of the aggrieved to contemplate whether there is an afterlife after death not only for the deceased but for everyone including the mourner.

Let's take the nature and interconnectivity of humor and worry or concern as examples. If two teenagers are ice skating together and one of them falls on her butt, that Emoji event or momentary signal is a cause for laughter even for the one sitting on the ice. If, however, a cry of anguish accompanied by the facial body language of suffering is let out by the fallen youngster, then humor takes a back seat and is replaced by concern, the degree of which depends upon the body image and sound of the words. Getting back to the teenager, if she's skating with her elderly grandmother and the latter falls on the ice, cries of anguish or not, it's an instantaneous Emoji symbol that causes immediate alarm. If, however, your brain identifies the person who falls as a bad character, it may evoke silent joy internally but feigned concern externally. It's important to note that the input-output function can oftentimes take place in less than a second. More about this significance of this later on.

Unlike elaborate explanatory written or verbal systemic efforts to make a point such as an article, essay, book or lecture, a single or simply the limited use of a few words or sayings can act as Emoji symbols which eliminate the need for detailed verbal or written explanation and expands its clarity. For example, "Aha!—I got it"! Or, "I caught you"! Or, "Ouch!—It hurts"— (either mentally or physically). Or, "Wow!—would you believe that China supplies 90 percent of garlic consumed in the United States?"

A sampling of other Emoji examples are as follows:

Sayings:

"Smile first thing in the morning. Get it over with!" W.C. Fields

"Sex is like fire; it can warm up your home or burn it down." Stephen L. DeFelice

An exasperated Charles Dickens lamenting to his literary colleague, Fyodor Dostoevsky: "Fyodor, I'm two people." Dostoevsky responds, "Charlie, is that all?!"

"We are restless, O' God, until we rest in thee." Saint Augustine

Winston Churchill's response to a friend seeking his advice upon the death of his mother-in-law: "Embalm, cremate, bury at sea. Take no chances!"

Auditory: Ocean waves pounding the surf create soothing sounds and a reflective state of mind; thunder, particularly when accompanied by lightning (a visual Emoji icon), evoke feelings of fear and the need to find shelter; a baby's cry sends out multiple signals of concern to the mother; music from the excitatory beat of rock and roll to the thrill of an operatic tenor's high C both augmented if heard and witnessed during a live performance (a visual Emoji icon).

One of my favorite quotes regarding the mystery and impact of sound was made by Charles Lamb, a famous essayist of the past, who wrote, "Not many sounds in life, and I include all urban and all rural sounds, exceed in interest a knock at the door."

Visual: a photo of a deceased loved one provokes sadness, teary eyes and a variety of memories of the past; a full moon offers a sense of beauty and metaphysical awe; the Mona Lisa makes one wonder what her smile was all about—and also about the genius of the left-handed artist, Leonardo Da Vinci himself and, to those who are romantically inclined, the nature of their relationship.

Olfactory: the smell of smoke alerts one to the possibility of fire somewhere close by; the smell of food cooking stimulates the appetite and the desire to taste what's giving off the odor; flatulence or passing gas, with or without the sound and odor, is a cause of embarrassment or laughter by the perpetrator or recipient, or both, depending on the circumstances.

Gustatory: the joy of consuming authentic, giant Beluga caviar from the sturgeons of the Caspian Sea along with a great champagne (no vodka, please!).

Body language: There are untold numbers of Emoji body language signals the expression of which are due to other stimuli. Bad news? The body slumps. Good news? The eyes light up. Bored or tired? Both yawn-producers. Disbelief? The eyes roll and the jaws drop.

Feelings: As with body language, there are untold numbers of Emoji signals which respond to stimuli such as pain, smell, depression, anxiety, the serenity of a beautiful sunset, the thrill of a slugfest boxing match, anger, sadness, stress, joy, pride, love and camaraderie. It is an uncommon Emoji experience that is not accompanied by some type of feeling.

Silence: Surprisingly, there is little research on the silence Emoji: meditation as a way to communicate with the deeper self and also, as with prayer, with something higher or spiritual; resolving problems and coming up with creative ideas. One definition of a friend is someone in whose presence one can remain comfortably silent.

Drugs: From approved prescription pharmaceuticals to recreational drugs which chemically alter the way the brain positively or negatively reacts to virtually all internal and external Emoji perception of signals. We currently have a cultural blindspot to the enormous downside of this trend.

Intuition, Extrasensory Perception or ESP and the Sixth Sense are natural epistemological phenomena which do not involve the obvious use of words.

In conclusion, all epistemological systems are faulty particularly when addressing the probability of the existence of a transcendental being or personal god. A more credible and relevant system is desperately needed. It's proposed that the Emoji Brain is that system. For religious educational advocates it is mandatory, therefore, to arm yourself with the detailed and working knowledge supporting this system before venturing out into the world to argue the case of the existence of a personal god.

Chapter 3

THE HUMAN TRANSCENDENTAL SEARCH

All people in all cultures have built in their brains the general human quality of searching for things from ways to avoid or eliminate suffering, finding food and shelter and a mate to be with to searching for small things such as the car key or lipstick in a woman's pocketbook. Also included in this array is the search for *transcendental experiences. The latter can be defined as the universal search for something beyond the normal human daily experience such as the existence of life after death.* The latter is unequivocally a natural property of the brain which existence defies scientific or any explanation except, as you will see—that of the Emoji Brain.

Before we go on, though you may have heard otherwise, we simply do not know what truly goes on in the mind of all humans. Yes, there are innumerable published descriptions of what goes on but they are all— and I mean all— extremely limited in scope. The only way to find out is to conduct a worldwide survey in representative sample populations in multiple cultures asking questions regarding what people think about life and the afterlife, which, in a practical sense, is not doable. Also, even if logistically doable, for a number of reasons, surveys are by nature extremely ineffective, as we have learned in the last U.S. presidential election. So, at least in the foreseeable future, we will never know.

But, to repeat and emphasize, what we do know is that all cultures, in one form or another, have ways to address the transcendental enigma which phenomenon is in the human brain and, therefore, natural. Before reviewing the broad variety of religious and other transcendental groups from large hierarchical ones to sprouting local, independent ones, the first step is to take a quick peek of what we are dealing with—and that's people. What is the core nature of *Homo sapiens* and how do individuals in a broad variety of cultures, from large to small and as far as we know, address the nature of an afterlife existence?

Let's begin with the marvels of modern photojournalism and its coverage of nature and the creatures of animal life from the African Serengeti to the Mariana Trench, the deepest point in all our oceans. What our gutsy, extremely patient photojournalists have clearly and objectively demonstrated are five fundamental activities among animals: killing others, then eating the captured prey, then resting and then having sex to reproduce their species. The fifth is seeking power either on a one-on-one basis or with a group. Sound familiar? We certainly fully share these characteristics for we are all animals!

And unless modern technology will soon alter the minds of earth's citizens, it will be a while before human nature changes. I am reminded of the Greek fable of the Scorpion and the Frog. There was a male frog on one side of a large pond who was about to cross to the other side in response to the irresistible love call of his lady friend. As he was about to enter the water, a scorpion approached him and asked whether he could hop a ride on his back to the other side. The frog replied, "Mr. Scorpion, are you nuts? You'll sting and poison me and I'll die." The scorpion replied, "You are the one who's nuts. If I sting you, we will both sink and drown and die for sure because scorpions can't swim." The frog paused, thought a bit, bought the argument and said, "Ok, hop on." Halfway across the pond the scorpion, out of the blue, stung him. The frog, astounded and befuddled, asked, "Why did you do that? Now we're both going to die." The scorpion, somewhat puzzled himself, apologetically replied, "I couldn't help it, Mr. Frog. It's in my nature!"

Homo sapiens is a political creature that lives in groups. With its highly developing brain, humans recognized that they needed rules to control the unfettered expression of the five innate qualities in order to live harmoniously in social communities of various types by creating customs, laws, religious guidelines and all sorts of other rules. They created arbitrary, empirical categories such as good, evil, moral, ethics and defined them according to the values of the culture. Thus casting unwanted newborn babies on a garbage heap was acceptable in pagan Rome but not so in Christian Rome. In Catholicism monogamy is the rule but in Islam, polygamy is limited to four wives.

I am not at all being cynical, but it's critical to note that today's anti-god and anti-religion forces frequently and arbitrarily employ the fuzzy words, moral and ethical—and they are fuzzy—as guidelines to proper behavior in an attempt to compete with religious-based ones and, by doing so, diminish the need and role of religion in society. Thus they heavily employ, using the elaborate use of words, reason and science as the standard to judge what is right or wrong behavior and not the Ten Commandments or the Sermon on the Mount or the Five Pillars of Islam. Not infrequently, either term is used as a way—advocates even deceive themselves—to add an aura of profundity when trying to make a point. Thus, how often have you heard something akin to, "This is a serious moral and ethical issue that we must resolve?" The problem is that the two terms aren't clearly defined simply because there is no standard definition due to the inadequacy of the words used to make the case. Ask yourself what's moral, what's ethical and what's the difference between the two, and you'll get the point. Don't be fooled by such prevalent verbal trickery.

An example of one currently, highly influential school of morality or ethics first promulgated by the brilliant Italian philosopher, Cesare Beccaria, and made mainstream by Jeremy Bentham and subsequent brilliant advocate, John Stuart Mill, utilitarianism, is extensively applied in medicine. Its primary credo is that a society should make sure that the greatest good or happiness be available to the greatest number of its populace and relegates minority groups to a lower status. Not too long ago I had dinner with an exceptionally bright utilitarian medical ethicist (the term medical moralist is rarely used which, in itself, adds to the confusion) who told me about a meeting he'd attended with a number of his colleagues on the importance of promoting legal euthanasia. They believe that with our exploding aging population we will have too many non-functioning old timers for our resources to handle, and it will be necessary to establish a national policy of euthanasia which will include even those who are of sound mind. It's an "ethical" form of triage commonly used in warfare with wounded soldiers on the battlefield where first treatment priority is given to the less severely wounded so that they can survive and, thereby, are able to return to fight the enemy again. Though in warfare where the rules are different and this policy is understandable, there's no doubt that Jesus would not agree on this policy regarding the elderly.

The unequivocal conclusion is that all moral-ethical systems are imperfect constructs based on written explanations employing the extensive use of words and sadly faulty. I believe it was Aristotle, who, after he wrote Ethics, his Magnus opus on ethics, regarding the soundness of his conclusions, confessed, "It's just too big to see."

Now let's take a look at how Eastern and Western civilizations perceive life after death. *What is striking is that much of the perception of the afterlife is based on the universal human experience of mental and physical suffering in this life.* Wise old Socrates counseled, "Be kind, for everyone you meet is fighting a hard battle." Centuries later and echoing Socrates is, what I believe is a Navajo tribal saying, "Do not judge a man until you have walked in his moccasins for two moons."

To be sure there are those who believe that fear of death, a national tragedy or the hope to be eternally with their loved ones and other impulses are psychologic factors behind afterlife-beliefs. But, bottom line, these do not nearly tell the entire story.

Regarding the Eastern and Western worlds what truly puzzles me are the stark differences of their perception of an afterlife. Though to be sure there are substantial overlapping gray zones, the Eastern cultures are almost entirely based on polytheistic mythology while the Western ones are a mixture heavily employing the added use of reason and monotheism in Christianity. Also, many definitions of life and afterlife in Eastern religions are impressively and mysteriously vague and open to various interpretations.

So let's start with the mysterious East.

HINDUISM

There appear to be nearly as many gods in Hinduism as the population of India! Bottom line, life is suffering and one goes through reincarnations or metempsychosis or a series of coming back to life in various biological forms until one reaches the final stage of Karma which opens the door to Moskva or Nirvana, the stage of the afterlife where suffering and desire, the cause of such suffering, are no more. The definitive nature of the afterlife self, however, is not clear.

BUDDHISM

Gautama Buddha was a Hindu heretic who substantially modified some of core Hinduism beliefs but retained many of them such as reincarnation and Nirvana but, unlike in Hinduism, there is no self after death but there is a state where the suffering due to reincarnation and individual desire is eliminated. Once more, though it is generally assumed that there is no life after death there is some type of "state" which continues. And, once more, the imprecise use of words prevents us from knowing about the nature of such a state.

CONFUCIANISM

Kong-zi, or Confucius, the latter name given to him by the Romans, was primarily concerned with adapting to this life of suffering and although he did not promote the existence of an afterlife, he did not deny it. He believed that one's ancestors had an impact on the lives of the living which bespeaks of an afterlife. When Confucius was asked by one of his disciples, "May I ask about death?" he answered, "You do not understand even life. How can you understand death?" And he, in an almost entire solitary state, mourned his mother's death for a three- year period. And it's difficult to conceive that he did not communicate with her thereby indicating his belief in a personal afterlife.

JUDAISM

Judaism is perhaps the first major monotheistic religion though there were bits of polytheistic beliefs such as with Moloch and Aron's golden calf.

Many of you will be surprised to learn that there is an unresolved debate in Judaism whether there is a life after death though periodic mentions of hell and heaven are mentioned in the Old Testament. The fact that Elijah never died and soared directly to heaven in a chariot supports the belief in an afterlife. Also, in the New Testament it's mentioned that that there were two Jewish authoritative groups, the Sadducees who believed that there is no such life and the Pharisees who did.

CHRISTIANITY

Catholicism is the first and largest of all Christian religions. Its doctrine is clearly and impressively spelled out as can be expected of any religion offering a guiding path for the living and what follows in the afterlife. The revolutionary new news is that each human being maintains his or her individuality after death. Though many will quibble on this point, its fundamental premise is similar to the Eastern religions— suffering is the natural human condition and this religion, like the others, offers ways to handle it while living. There is Heaven, Hell and Purgatory in between. Heaven is the state of the Beatific Vision, the eternal beholding of the image of God; Hell is where one spends an eternity burning in relentless flames and Purgatory is where one who was not sufficiently evil to deserve eternal punishment, yet not good enough to immediately enter heaven and, as a compromise, must spend some time doing penance there before being permitted to enter through its gates.

Other Christian sects such as the Eastern Orthodox Church and a number of Protestant ones believe that a loving God would not permit such cruel eternal punishment in Hell and, therefore, limit a person's stay there for a period proportional to the sin after which one can then enter heaven. The nature of Heaven, however, differs among the sects and, frankly speaking, more often than not, is not clearly defined.

On a personal note, I—and I'm sure a number of you, too—would welcome the existence of Purgatory because we don't have a snowball's chance in Hell, pardon the pun, to directly enter the pearly gates of Heaven!

ISLAM

In a sense, Islam can be viewed as a form of Protestantism, a breakaway from Catholicism. It still maintains the belief in a single God and a heaven. Regarding the latter, however, it's of a different nature where the elusive, persistently sought after physical and mental pleasures of a human existence on earth are finally found and eternally fulfilled.

ERSATZ RELIGIONS

What I primarily mean by ersatz religions, once more because of the limitations in the use of words, is impossible to clearly define. They are non-organized religious or other types of groups based on strong emotional feelings of support permeated by a broad variety of cultural and emotional beliefs. This is, coupled with a prevalent absence of reason and scientific input, much akin to the mystical dynamics of Eastern religions. All are searching for something transcendental. Such entities are gaining ground in America while our large, organized Christian religions are contemporaneously losing it.

These ersatz religions are of various types most of which, unlike the traditional ones, are doctrineless largely based on evoking uplifting emotions which connect to God. There are the megachurches and multiple small single, independent parishes as seen, for example, in the Black and Hispanic communities—a few of which I have personally visited and participated in their services. What has particularly attracted my attention is the emergence of entertainment religion primarily driven by rock concert-like formats to large crowds with strobe lights and other excitatory musical techniques and songs accompanied by Christian lyrics. There may be a larger message in this emerging phenomenon. During the 8th century it's believed that a Catholic monk who became Pope Gregory composed a multitude of songs praising God written in Latin famously known as the Gregorian chants. Though most of the people in the countries did not understand Latin, these songs had a tremendous unifying effect on the Catholic religion. What fascinates me was that the combination of the human voice itself and the melodies without an understanding of the Latin lyrics had such an overwhelming religious impact.

As a young doctor, I treated a number of opera singers some of whom were the great ones. I, of course, was in love with opera and with the power and symbolic messages of music in general. I studied its history and agreed with Plato who wrote, "Any change in styles of music is always followed by change in the most fundamental laws of state" which brings to mind Jacob Burckhardt's observation that, "Culture precedes art." To summarize: Culture precedes art or music and music is a harbinger of a change in the state.

Other manifestations of what I consider ersatz religious movements are the explosion of therapists who deal with millions of unsettling states of mind, the search for nutritional paths to health and longevity, and the consumption of enormous quantities of recreational and regulatory approved pharmaceutical drugs. And let's not forget spiritualism.

RITUALS

Regarding rituals, virtually all groups, whether religious or not, from the primitive to the complex, have rituals that celebrants follow in order to establish common, uniform unifying rules for all to follow in order to help find what they're searching for.

The Hindus, by the multi- millions, bathe in the Ganges River which they believe to be the actual Goddess, Ganga, in order to end the cycle of reincarnation. The Christians, either singly or in small groups, undergo baptism in order to abolish original sin committed by Adam and Eve.

We are immersed in a world of myriads of simple and complex secular and religious rituals from how the dinner table should be set before saying grace to knocking on wood for good luck; from circumcision to exorcism; from the marriage ceremony along with the symbolic binding marriage ring and from attending Catholic Mass to the Islamic mandate to pray five times a day while facing Mecca.

It's critical to note that whatever the ritual, secular or religious, it is a search for a purpose.

PHILOSOPHICAL-THEOLOGICAL ARGUMENTS

Before the scientific revolution, philosophy, the attempt to discover the truth regarding what life is all about by employing reason by the elaborate use of words, largely concentrated on theology in the attempt to both prove the existence and nature of the biblical God. The impact of the scientific revolution a few centuries ago turned philosophy's primary focus to reason and science still, however, relying on the elaborate use of words. Here I'd like to review the major arguments for the existence of God or Supreme Being based on old and even some modern philosophical arguments.

The "big three" philosophical arguments, though there is inevitable overlapping, are categorized as ontological, cosmological and teleological. There are other less persuasive ones such as the moral argument which I'd like to first address because it has, in my opinion, not been sufficiently explored. Also, I would like to expand its scope and include it into what I call the Altruistic Argument which we'll discuss later on.

Simply put, the moral argument goes as follows: Since some form of morality exists in all cultures, and may I add that that means in the brains of their inhabitants, there must be something transcendental that put it there. What is lacking, as mentioned before, is a common definition of the term, *moral,* let alone of the puzzling left-out word of these arguments, namely, *ethical.*

So let's begin with the moral-ethical argument by attempting to define the moral or morality term: it deals with general principles of what individual cultures consider good or bad behavior. For example, a soldier should not desert his post during battle or one should not tell a lie or cheat. The ethicist takes this theoretical principle and applies it to real life situations. Let's say parents with limited income cheat on their income taxes—which is telling a lie—in order to have enough money to send their children to vocational school or college. This act would be considered an unethical one by the modern professional ethicist but not so by hard working people. In fact, it would be considered the right or ethical thing to do. Ask yourself whose side you would take. If a rich man, however, cheats on his taxes, that's another story, and generally would be considered an unethical act. Or, is it otherwise since the government would waste his money on inevitable unethical acts?

And here's another prevalent dilemma: the individual versus the general good. When does an individual person's good supersede that of a larger one like one's country? As a learning exercise think about the subject of *diversity* which national emotional controversy exceeds even that of Intelligent Design. What is the fundamental moral principle supporting diversity—write it down!—and what are some of its ethical applications which are clearly based on the principle? We know, for example, that the application of diversity leads to all kinds of quotas. We also know that there are quotas that benefit the individual and weaken the country and vice versa. It's not the purpose of this book to delve into this subject but I raise the issue to encourage you to go through this exercise as a learning experience to appreciate the limited moral- ethical approach to human behavior.

Though, however, there are many perplexing gray zones in the ethical applications of moral principles one thing is abundantly clear: *No society can tolerate the majority of its people being liars, deserters, thieves or murderers!* Vague, however, as the particular moral-ethical individual applications are, there is a universal commonality underlying them in all cultures. But, to repeat, the gray zones of cultural values prevent them from being universally applied with precision.

In my opinion, there is, however, another universal characteristic of the brain that is less vague, more consistent and unequivocal—and that quality is altruism, a term which was coined by the French philosopher, Auguste Comte, during the nineteenth century. It's a derivation of the Italian word, *altrui,* which means "to others". Unfortunately, there are many definitions and, as with moral and ethical terms, they are frustratingly vague. I would, therefore, like to propose a simple definition which most would, without hesitation, understand. *Altruism is a frame of mind that makes people want or feel the need to help other people.* Thus a person responds to another in need of help. This, as with most definitions, is open to criticism. But the Emoji Brain knows it when it observes a multitude of altruistic acts during a lifetime.

Most definitions erroneously state that the person rendering the help does so without consideration of any benefit to him or her. That, I must say, is a classic yet unrecognized error. I know that when I help people I, I'm sure as with others, feel good and feeling good is a personal benefit. Altruism, like friendship, is undoubtedly a two-way street.

29

It's interesting to note that those who are anthropomorphically inclined sincerely believe that many animals are altruistic, often citing examples of dolphins helping drowning humans to safe territory and a single case of a leopard that helped a baby baboon. Though this may be true to some degree, the evidence is weak. It's important to note that the chasm of differences between man and animals of characteristics such as altruism and others including thought and complex language immensely adds to the uniqueness of the human brain. One must wonder why there is no in-between species that is closer to us. There is a message to think about behind this absence.

Finally, if you think about it, altruism encompasses a broad spectrum of human characteristics such as love, moral-ethical applications and heroism, among others.

I believe that combining the more definitive concept of altruism with the current vague moral argument into the broader more concrete and credible Altruistic Argument will strengthen its support of a Supreme Being which can be integrated into the ontological argument.

Now back to the Big three arguments: Ontology deals with the concept that the idea of God is, in one way or another, present in our brains; cosmology deals with the concept of what makes things change and teleology deals with the concept that all things in the universe, including we mere mortals, have a definite purpose.

Regarding the ontological argument, it was first proposed by a spirited St. Anselm during the middle ages. He was born in Italy and somehow ended up in England as Archbishop of Canterbury tangling with a couple of monarchs. The following is a description of his clever but faulty argument which, though rejected by Thomas Aquinas and others, started the ontological movement influencing Descartes, Leibniz and though he would probably deny it, Kant.

Anselm's reasoning is as follows: "We define God as a being which nothing greater can be thought. Now, there is in the mind the idea of such a being. But such a being must exist outside the mind; for, if it did not, it would not be that than which nothing greater can be thought. Therefore, God exists not only in the mind, as an idea, but also outside the mind as a reality."

Though it's not my intent to critique his argument and for you to tackle the reasoning, the basic fault as is common with other philosophies, having an idea about something doesn't make it real. *Anselm's groundbreaking contribution is the emphasis that the thought of something transcendental such as God is in the human brain along with other natural qualities such as altruism, morality, love and hate.*

Let's now jump to the 17th century and Descartes, who is considered the father of modern philosophy. He proposed two theories on the existence of God but we'll review the principal one. If you recall, in his epistemology he first doubted his existence but tried to prove it with *Cogito ergo sum,* or *I think therefore I am.* After having first allegedly proven his own existence, he writes, "Of the ideas which I find in my mind, some arise from external causes and others from the mind itself. Now, among the ideas which I possess is the idea of God, that idea of a most perfect Being. This idea, however, cannot have been produced by me; for the fact that I doubt proves that I am an imperfect being, and an imperfect being cannot cause that which is most perfect. He alone Who is Himself endowed with all perfections can produce in my mind the idea of a most perfect Being. Therefore, from the idea of God which I possess, I am warranted in concluding that God exists."

Though Anselm and Descartes arrived at the same ontological conclusion, Anselm maintains that the brain, itself, takes us to the conclusion that God exists, while Descartes maintains that God, himself, actively put the idea in our brains. Splitting hairs or not?

Let's now visit the cosmological argument which deals with change and what causes it. The pre-Socratic philosophers were enamored with the nature of change, a representative example being the positions of Heraclitus versus Parmenides. Heraclitus maintained that everything changes while Parmenides maintained that nothing does. If, for example, one dunked his foot in a river, then took it out and then dunked it into it again, Heraclitus would maintain that it's a different river. Parmenides, incredulous and staring at his colleague would say, "Heraclitus, are you out of your mind. It's the same damn river!" Which side would you take?

The standard cosmological arguments originated from the mind of the inescapable intellect of Aristotle. He maintained that things change and logically concluded that something must cause or move them to change.

31

But everything is changing here and now at a specific point in time and, therefore, something that is not changing itself must be the prime agent of change or mover, and that must be God. This god, of course, is not a personal one.

Aquinas accepted this philosophic concept and concluded that the prime mover is a personal god or that of Catholicism.

Now to teleology, the most easily understood and acceptable among all the arguments: Simply put, teleology maintains that everything in nature has or serves a purpose. Thus rain makes plants to grow; plants make oxygen for all to breathe and oxygen makes us live. Bone marrow makes blood cells and the heart pumps them to the lungs for oxygenation and then to all body tissues to deliver oxygen and also nutrients. Love exists between a man and a woman to join them together in order to bring a child into the world and propagate the race.

A first major teleologist was, once more, our old inescapable friend, Aristotle, who argued that everything in nature exists for a purpose which assumes universal acts of intention. Aquinas, as one of his ways to prove the existence of God, accepts this teleological argument and takes it to a higher level. He believes that since all of nature has a purpose or intent then there must be supreme intelligence to have created all the governing forces which make it happen. And, it logically follows, that this intelligent being is a personal god.

The most famous and oft-attacked analogy supporting the teleological argument was effectively promoted by the English philosopher, William Paley, in his book, *Natural Theology*, published in 1802. In it he compares a watch to the world and the watchmaker to God. If someone were walking in a field and came upon a watch what would he think about on what he discovered? First of all, somebody—an individual—lost the watch. It just wasn't there on its own. Then, if he dismantled it, he would discover how all the integral parts were intelligently assembled or designed by someone for the purpose of telling accurate time. As an analogy, nature is also a complex structure with multiple functions, and it follows that there must be a transcendent watchmaker or designer, or God.

This argument is so persuasive that lots of philosophers and others who are not sympathetic to the watchmaker message have been energized using lots of elaborate word arguments and faulty assumptions to discredit the Paley analogy such as nature is not a man-made machine.

Speaking of analogies, what if you and a philosopher were walking together in the fields and came upon a Tootsie Roll or Nutella bar. You would know that some specific company conceived of and produced the Roll or bar—and even be tempted to taste it— while the philosopher would make the argument that we can never know and not be sure of its contents and tasting it won't help to find out. Go figure!

An example of the intensity of this antagonism occurred in America on whether the subject of Intelligent Design, that there is purpose in nature, should be taught in our schools along with the theory of evolution. Though, on the surface, this seemed to be a reasonable objective but, and justifiably so, it was read by its opponents as a way to sneak God back into the classrooms which resulted in a huge, emotion-laden countermovement and was soundly defeated. This confrontation is a clear and telling example of the anti-God and anti-religious antagonism of our times.

The inescapable conclusion is that it is in our nature to constantly search for things from the mundane to the transcendental. Included in the latter is the search for some type of afterlife.

Chapter 4

SCIENCE AND THE UNIVERSE

In our technology-cyberspace explosion era there are untold numbers of emerging experts in virtually every area of life from what we eat to sex to politics and to the existence and nature of God. Regarding God, among such experts are philosophers, religious and secular intellectuals and scientists. An influential community of scientists preaches the doctrines of atheism and agnosticism but the majority of the latter do so only half-heartedly and deep-down tend toward the atheistic pole. Scientists, or non-scientists who employ scientific information, generally rely on both the physical dynamics of the Universe and Biological Evolution in wordy attempts at reason to support their arguments. And, that which is critical to note, is the paucity of recognized leaders capable of effective rebuttals which can then be transmitted to key pro-God educational leaders.

Regarding atheistic arguments which conclude that an intelligent transcendental being or God does not exist, it's essential to particularly note that, as we shall see, such arguments, by necessity, are all faulty. You, therefore, may justifiably wonder why they are increasingly being trumpeted and accepted by much of the media and academic communities.

One principal reason is that, spurred by the modern deluge of information, we are being captured by the age-old social phenomenon of the Argument from Authority. If so-and-so says this is true or good for you, then it must be true or good for you. Now on the practical level of everyday living, we, of course, must rely on some authority to help us wade through the daily formidable information river of life. If your professor, an authority, teaches that the speed of light is about 186,000 miles per second and can circumnavigate the approximate 25,000- mile circumference of the equator in 7.5 seconds, you can comfortably assume it's true. If your doctor, also an authority, tells you that your blood sugar is high, that you are diabetic and need medication, you understandably accept it as an unfortunate fact. Then there are the myriad daily lessons and messages of life to be learned depending on where one's life is situated and heading. Who knows about life better— a man running a family construction business managing personnel, meeting payroll, handling legal matters, maintaining and expanding his market in the face of fierce competition or a tenured, sheltered professor of mathematics or philosophy?

When, however, one ventures into matters of the existence and nature of God, be they positive or negative, there is no professor or doctor-like authority but speculators only. We are all equal. Regarding atheism, this extremely critical fact is being totally ignored when so-called authorities communicate under the umbrella of the Argument of Authority. *They are, without question, no more qualified than any other non-authority to guess what or who God may or may not be.* Thus when the superb scientific mind of Albert Einstein concludes that there is no personal god to meet in the afterlife, it carries no more weight than when the great evangelist, Billy Graham, concludes that in his afterlife he's going where Jesus is. Now many of you will, without a second thought, instinctively disagree with this observation, and you may be right, favoring scientific opinion: and you also may not be. Let's then move forward and first explore the world of science starting with a bit of history.

It's claimed that the philosopher, Thales of Miletus, is the father of science. He lived in what is now Western Turkey about 2,600 years ago. He eschewed mythological belief stressing the importance of repeated observations of nature to discover things. As an example of the times, it's said that the Greeks would rather debate on how many teeth were in a human mouth instead of asking someone to open it and actually count them! About a century later, the philosopher, Anaxagoras, focused on outer space speculating that humans on earth may have originated from there which some have called *panspermia*. A couple of centuries later, the Greek astronomer, Aristarchus, postulated the heliocentric theory, that the Sun, and not the Earth, is the center of our solar system.

Scientific progress moved slowly until a few centuries ago when it picked up speed and brought us to the marvels of modern discovery from learning about the behavior of microscopic cellular genes to the existence of enormous, brilliant quasars at the outer rims of our galaxy, the Milky Way.

During this phase attempts were made to establish the disciplined rules of scientific experimentation in order to objectively validate or invalidate a hypothesis or to answer a question based on the results of laboratory and other types of experimental studies. The result of this effort was what is now called the *scientific method* which spells out the specific steps needed to be taken in order to prove or disprove an idea or hypothesis. For example, to answer the question whether a five pound rock falls at the same or greater speed than a one pound one, one must go to a height, drop them from the same level at the same time and measure which one strikes the ground first. For the record, both will hit the ground at the same time but a feather will fall far behind. If a patient tells his doctor that he's experiencing polyuria, polyphagia and polydipsia—all manifestations of diabetes—the doctor must request a measurement of his blood and urine glucose or sugar to confirm his diagnosis or hypothesis.

Now let's look at how the *scientific method* is employed when asked the question, "Does God exist?" Where to begin? Stumped? So am I. There are no rocks or feathers. There is no patient or blood sugar test. There is nothing to measure!

The uncontestable truth is that the scientific method, the golden rule of science, cannot be applied to the existence or non-existence of a transcendental being or God.

There is another uncontestable truth which not only scientists or intellectuals who rely on science when communicating from their pulpits ignore or are ignorant of: it's what I call the *Mystery of Why*.

Though I'm reluctant to re-enter the quagmire of epistemology, I have no choice. When we view a thing or event, we do so from three aspects; namely that it is, what it is and why it is. Let's, as an example, look at gravity, one of the four basic forms of energy. We know that it is and something about what it is by being able to measure what it does. Yes, the rock falls to earth but we haven't the slightest idea why it doesn't go upwards instead of downwards. Why does gravity do what it does is as unanswerable as why does a zygote, about the size of period, become a baby. The Mystery of Why permeates all that exists.

We will deal more with the Mystery of Why in subsequent pages.

THE UNIVERSE

When discussing the nature of the Universe, one cannot help but starting with the Big Bang, Higgs boson and Hubble's expanding Universe. But before we go on, and lest he be forgotten, let's talk about a little known Belgian scientist Catholic priest, Georges Lemaitre. In 1927 he, as a forerunner of the Big Bang postulated—not proved—that the Universe was created from the explosion of a single primeval atom or "Cosmic Egg" at single point in time and, in addition, that the universe was expanding. As a young physician, I became aware of the phenomenon of who gets credit for an original thought or a discovery having personally experienced it. There's the Meucci- Graham Bell one regarding who discovered the telephone; the Darwin-Wallace one regarding evolution; the Leibniz-Newton controversy on the discovery of calculus when it was the Greek, Archimedes, the Eureka guy in the bathtub, who first came up with the concept. Regarding Leibniz, I recently read that he, before Einstein, believed that space-time was not fixed, but relative.

Getting back to the Belgian priest and the Cosmic Egg, Pope Pius XII saw this as a unique opportunity to scientifically support the story of Creationism as described in Genesis and wanted to employ it in the Church's educational armamentarium. Lemaitre, however, was fearful because he, along with his colleagues, ostensibly believed that science and religion are two distinct entities and should not be mingled. But there was more to the story than that explanation which still plays an understandably powerful role in today's science-religion conflict. It's the historic reality that, generally speaking, organized religion has been the enemy of science. The story of Galileo and the Inquisition is often used as the classic example of the conflict. Some believe that the fear of this event along with others such as the burning at the stake of Giordano Bruno who, like Anaxagoras, believed in panspermia and other heretical concepts, so frightened potential scientific minds in southern Europe that it discouraged them from practicing their profession. As a result, it was in northern Europe where modern science blossomed.

THE POPE'S REPORT ON THE BIG BANG

Let's imagine that the first American pope, Pope Xavier, wasted no time. It was only a month after he was elected by the papal conclave when he summoned his former student Bishop Jonathan Bradley to the Vatican. The bishop was a young rising extremely bright star in the Church gifted with exceptional communication skills. He was also well versed and respected in astrophysics.

It was a beautiful Roman sunny day and Vatican City was pregnant with visitors. Observing the visitors from his window, the pope commented, "Jonathan, I used to love to stroll alone through the streets of Rome, but God has now taken that privilege away."

They then sat down for a light lunch— a mixed, room-temperature seafood platter with a side plate of escarole with a tasty dressing. Regarding the white wine, the pope decided to limit the supply to one glass each in order to maintain their mutual acuity.

He began, "During my many years in the United States, I've watched the influence of the Catholic Church and the general belief in our biblical God inexorably on the road of decline. Yes, Jonathan, I know there are many reasons for this decline and all are somehow directly or indirectly related to technology. Now that I have some real clout, I want to do something with real impact to fight this destructive beast. And I have an idea that I've been thinking about for the past few years."

The bishop, with a broad smile and curious eyes, slowly sipped on the wine and said, "Father Xavier, I like what I hear, and I'm all ears. So go ahead."

It was the pope's turn to take a sip, after which he paused and gazed toward the window as if in a trance. He then mentally returned to the table and, in determined tones, proclaimed, "Jonathan, something very big— and I mean big— has to be done in order to energize our thought leaders in a crusade to bring back God in national discussions. I'm not talking about Catholicism but, as the first step, a persuasive argument—now hear this! — based primarily on science. You see, when I witnessed, decades ago, the

Catholic Universities turning to secularism and scientism, two connected expanding movements, I knew we had lost our way because our Christian communities sat on their asses— forgive me God—and had no effective counterarguments. Mentioning Jesus, let alone God, in our major Catholic universities had begun to become a rarer and even unwelcomed act."

He then glanced at the ceiling and in stentorian tones, beseechingly pleaded, "Father in Heaven, please forgive me again but your Son, Jesus, once said that 'the truth shall make you free.'"

The bishop smiled to himself observing the theatrical side of the pope that had played a major role in winning over the papacy. He also wondered why he was asking God, the Father, for forgiveness and didn't have to wait for the answer.

"Though spreading the message of love is the primary message that Jesus and others in the Bible preached, it has not been enough to turn the tide in America. As you are well aware, it has recently been tried and was an abysmal failure as the scientism-secularism forces continued to grow unopposed."

He turned to his wine again, sipped away, and once more in stentorian tones and with fire in his eyes, exclaimed, "Jonathan, we must fight fire with fire!"

The young bishop was tempted to ask the pope what he had in mind but decided to remain silent and let things flow. Their wine glasses were almost empty. Pope Xavier now changed his mind and pressed a button on the table. The door opened and a young man entered. The pope, politely and with respect, asked, "Young man, would you kindly bring us some more of this delightful white wine. Is it from a local winery?"

The young man, visibly proud and with expanded chest, replied, "Yes, Father Xavier, it's from my father's vineyard."

"Well, send both of our sincere thanks to your father for this wonderful surprise."

The young man's eyes were beaming with pride. He left and returned with the bottle of wine in hand, showed the pope the label, poured the nectar almost to the brim, and still with an expanded chest, departed.

The bishop then observed, "Father Xavier, Jesus would have been proud of you. That was an act of love, a small but powerful one. That young man can't wait to tell his father, family and friends. It will be recorded in the family history archives."

After hearing these words the pope seemed momentarily relaxed. He smiled and said, "Now let's get to the big battle for the souls of mankind."

They hadn't yet touched their lunch when the pope began, "It's the Lemaitre's Cosmic Egg. I want to know what laid it. We must boldly crack its shell and see what's in it. You see, the Big Bang is now accepted as holy writ in scientific, educational and media circles. But how this happened has never been fully explored in detail. And, God forbid if anyone raises the possibility that God might have done it for he or she would be laughed out of town. It's anti-intellectualism and anti-religion in the extreme. Yet there's little doubt in my mind that if we vigorously analyze the Big Bang and the nature of the Universe, we will logically conclude that, among the reasonable possibilities, a transcendental, intelligent being is one of them. And I emphasize reasonable.

"Father Bradley, *che ne pensi*? What do you think?"

There followed a slight pause and both slowly took to their lunch. The bishop was obviously in heavy thought and the pope wisely remained silent to give his brilliant mind time to sort things out.

The bishop then broke the silence by saying, "It's risky and might backfire." He then hesitated for a moment and then said, "I'll take that back. It may be a brilliant idea. I'm not denying the risk but here's what I have in mind, and I'm willing to be captain of the ship. I'll put together a group of bright minds composed of scientists and non-scientists including religious intellects. Let's say about seven of them which I find the optimum number in think tanks of this type. This, of course, will be done behind closed doors, and the final report will be given to you to determine what to do with it.

"Father Xavier, *che ne pensi?*"

The pope, without hesitation, replied, "You got a deal. How much time will it take?"

The bishop, also without hesitation, replied, "About sixty days. But I must remind you that these guys will not have their names listed on the report unless they agree to it. It all, of course, depends on the content of the report and what you want to do with it, if anything." Silence prevailed for a moment as they both took to the wine. The pope stood up, walked to the window and forlornly remarked, 'Oh, how I'd love to take a stroll around *bella Roma* today."

SUMMARY: COSMIC EGG REPORT

To Pope Julius Xavier
Re: Summary of Big Bang Theory Report: What Laid the Cosmic Egg?
Fr. Bishop Jonathan Bradley and others

Our approach was to ask and answer questions that we thought would be sufficient to at least reasonably speculate on what laid Lemaitre's Cosmic Egg. Our group employed a combination of the standard scientific method, disciplined reasoning and common sense. The latter is critical for it takes the dynamic human searching brain to where the scientific method (including mathematics and computational modeling) and disciplined, complex reasoning cannot go.

It should be pointed out that most of our technology to explore the Universe, including the Cosmic Egg, is woefully limited, and we must rely on our creative scientists to squeeze as much information as possible from such limited technology. For example, we must rely on the enormous 17-mile Hadron Collider to, within a fraction of a second, discover Higgs boson, a subatomic particle created after protons crash into each other at almost the speed of light, the few LIGO and Virgo centers, relying only on just a few brief beeps to detect gravitational waves from the collision of two giant black holes supporting Einstein's theory of relativity, telescopes to explore the galaxies and its contents and satellites attempting to communicate with celestial aliens. Regarding the latter, it is cleverly thought that one way to test for celestial plant life is to measure celestial fluorescent chlorophyll. Then there are the invisible dark matter and dark energy that we have to find. Father Xavier, the list of unknowns is long.

Though the existence of the Cosmic Egg and Big Bang are overwhelmingly accepted by the scientific community, there are those who are not so sure—and maybe they are right, but we don't think so. For example, the Law of Conservation of Mass and Energy holds that matter cannot either be created or destroyed. Another is that the speed of cosmic inflation after the Big Bang is believed to have exceeded the speed of light which speed in not—at least not yet—attainable in our Universe. But the laws of physics that currently exist in our Universe may have been different back then and still may be in some places particularly if there are parallel universes.

And finally, you will note that we do not mention God in our report because of the anticipated huge, negative reaction from the highly influential science and academic communities.

Given the aforementioned limitations, the following is the summary of the questions addressed and our responses to them:

1.   *What is the Cosmic Egg, What is the Big Bang, and What existed before the former and during the latter?* We don't know what the composition of the Cosmic Egg was except that it is estimated to be no bigger than a zygote or fertilized human egg and which contained within it all the future potential elements—every single atom!—of our current Universe including the human body. It's estimated by some that the Big Bang occurred about 13.8 billion years ago in a trillionth of a trillionth of a trillionth of a second and almost instantaneously formed and expanded the Universe by what is called cosmic inflation. And the Universe is still expanding today.

2.   *What existed before the Cosmic Egg and the Big Bang?* We simply don't know. Also, we don't know if the formation of the Cosmic Egg independently preceded the Big Bang or was part of a single process. But what we can reasonably assume is that something caused the entire process to happen. If, however, as some claim, nothing at all existed before, then the phenomenon is that of pure creation, i.e., making something out of nothing which physical possibility has yet been proven to exist but which claim, as you are well aware, is made in the Bible. If something existed before that caused both events, the phenomenon is, of course, not that of pure creation but some other type of mystery.

3.   *Where and what is the Universe expanding or heading to?* As with the Big Bang and where it came from, there is not a credible theory on where the Universe is heading.

4.   *What happened after the Cosmic Egg- Big Bang eruption up until today?* It's believed that after the Big Bang, the Universe was too hot to sustain

stable physical particles such as molecules but with the passing of time, matter such as atoms, molecules and other forms of matter such as stars and asteroids came to be ultimately resulting into evolution and the formation of the human brain and consciousness. Now we must turn again to epistemology, good old Aristotle, Paley's watch and the Tootsie roll and Nutella bar. Though philosophers will question our ability to determine cause-effect connections, we believe that most of mankind— maybe everyone except a couple of philosophers—from the primitive to the highly technologic will believe that "something" indeed caused the transformation of subatomic particles into stars and we humans.

Then the next question would be that of "entelechy" or what mysterious "principle" or "factor" in those particles made these conversions and all others in the Universe what they are. These phenomena and trillions of others are beyond mathematics and computational modeling. And forget about probability statistics. In conclusion, Father Xavier, we feel we let you down regarding our findings on what laid the Cosmic Egg but your guess is as good as ours. There is, however, some room for optimism. As we previously mentioned, many scientists and atheists among them believe that nothing existed before the Cosmic Egg and the Big Bang. If so, the event was an act of pure creation which supports a transcendental being. We strongly propose that the Vatican hold a conference with a group of distinguished scientists along with philosophers and theologians, agnostics and atheist among them, to courageously address the question, "What possible force or entity could have created the Cosmic Egg and the Big Bang?" Think about it.

Chapter 5

EVOLUTION

I remember well when it happened for it was the year that I was married and John F. Kennedy was elected President of the United States. I was leading a discussion session at my medical fraternity on evolution. What's interesting to note is that we, for reasons due to chance, had a quota system-approximately 1/3 Catholic, 1/3 Jewish and 1/3 Protestant members. A significant percentage of each group harbored some degree of Judeo-Christian religious beliefs and others not.

And, boy, did the sparks fly—not on the subject of the pros and cons of the various evolutionary theories but whether the biblical God was behind it. The passions of the anti-God faction clashed with the pro-God ones to such a degree that I shut down the discussion for we were getting nowhere. Unfortunately, with the passage of time and up until the present, this type of non-intellectual, highly charged emotional reaction to discussions on evolution has not changed constantly being fueled by proponents of each camp.

Before we go on let's take a quick walk through history up until our current era of exploding scientific discovery.

It makes a lot of sense to combine the subject of the origin of life with its evolution. It's puzzling why there were relatively few minds that tackled both concepts in depth. In pre-Socratic Greece some proposed the concept of spontaneous generation, that life arose from inanimate matter such as mud or water. It was, again, the two great philosophers, Plato and his student, Aristotle, the father of biology, who impacted evolutionary thought for centuries. Plato believed that organisms had a purpose and developed in the direction to what goal they were intended. A fish was made to swim, a bird to fly and a man to think. Aristotle proposed that life arose from inanimate matter according to a "scale of nature" with plants at the bottom of the scale and humans on the top, also each with specific goals or purposes.

With the oncoming of Catholicism, the Judeo-Christian belief that God created mankind permeated Western civilization until after the Renaissance. Men and women were created by an act of God and that was that. Then there appeared a number of men who attempted to analyze both concepts more objectively, and it was Lamarck during the 18th century who proposed the inheritance of acquired characteristics. Simply put, it is the impact of what living things encounter in their environments that are transmitted to their offspring, the most famous example being that a giraffe's neck grows in length because its food, the leaves, are growing higher and higher in the trees. It's interesting to note that a giraffe has the same number of vertebrae as we humans.

This thinking along with others such as the primordial soup or hylozoism theories more or less percolated along until the 19th century when Darwin and Wallace separately published their revolutionary theory of evolution which theory Herbert Spencer coined as the "Survival of the fittest."

Though the definitions are fuzzy, what followed was frequently labeled as Neo-Darwinism. Though Mendelian genetics was part of the thinking of the Darwinian-Wallace advocates, it was Neo-Darwinism, fueled by our genetic technologic advances, that broadened the concept of *survival of the fittest* based primarily on genetic mutations and secondarily how the environment impacts them. The thinking is that genetic mutations randomly occur by chance and based on such mutations the environment determines which organism should survive. There is no plan or purpose. All is due to randomness and chance. The advocates seem to ignore the pigeon hole principle and Ramsey's theorem which demonstrate that complete patternlessness is impossible. They also ignore the impact of epigenetics. Neo-Darwinism is clearly not a credible theory.

Then Lamarck made a recent comeback when, though the Greeks first thought of it, the field of epigenetics gained legitimacy. Epigenetics demonstrates that the environment, either within or without the body, either internal or external to the organism, can alter genetic expression and function without altering the genetic structure itself, and that this genetic expression can even be transmitted to future offspring. Thus methylation can alter the expression of certain genes and elevated temperatures can change the determination of sexual gender in certain animals.

The Biological Big Bang Theory and the Big Three Life-Giving Mysteries Questions

About 4.5 billion years ago the earth was born. Estimates on when and how life came to be range from a one-time event early on to multiple, episodic ones at successive intervals. There is certainly evidence based on molecular chirality and the physical structure of amino acids to support that, as with the Universe, a Biological Big Bang Theory regarding the creation of life was a single event. Whatever the case, whether due to a single or multiple event, one can safely assume that the origin of life is part of a similar process to achieve an intended goal or purpose.

It's interesting to note the rarely mentioned paucity of evidence regarding the causes of the three biggest mysteries on the origins and evolution of life. Whatever the reason, they are relatively absent from debates on evolution and yet present a highly promising opportunity to support the argument for the existence of a transcendental being.

The first is abiogenesis: How did animate or living matter originate from inanimate or nonliving matter? How did RNA and DNA self-replicate themselves?

The second is self-organization: How then did this living matter organize itself into biological systems in order to function, thrive and stay alive?

The third, not to be confused with the second, is emerging phenomena: How did simple organisms develop more complicated and sophisticated organ systems? How, for example, did the human brain evolve from a more primitive phase of evolution?

Now, these three questions present a unique and highly promising opportunity which will, at first, be soundly rejected by powerful secular forces, but on perseverance, will be found to be quite reasonable and difficult to reject. When educational courses on evolution are given in schools, it should be mandatory that these three questions be asked and possible answers addressed by the students. One quite reasonable, uncontestable and, may I add, scientific possibility is the existence of a transcendental being.

Though there is not a single theory supported by the scientific method or any other solid evidence regarding the causes of the origin and evolution of all life, there are some things such as the aforementioned abiogenesis, self-organization and emerging phenomena which are self-evident or sufficiently substantiated to accept. It is self-evident, for example, that dinosaurs were not our first life-form but there is sufficient evidence to substantiate that prokaryotes, single cell organisms without a nucleus such as bacteria, were among the first living organisms. After millions of years there then appeared eukaryote organisms which have more sophisticated cells containing, for example, nuclei. Then came the dinosaurs and all other trillions of forms and functions of life, including the appearance of the modern human and all of its activities from staying alive to being conscious and having feelings and thoughts.

Regarding science's credible answers to the big three life-giving mystery questions, they are nonexistent—not even close! The discovery of the causes is far beyond the scope of current standard scientific methods. To repeat, for reasons that specialists in individual and group behavior can best address, these critical questions are seldomly adequately addressed in evolutionary debates but have remained expertly and oftentimes intentionally buried from analysis let alone even a mentioning. This pattern must be abolished for the scientific discussions regarding the possible answers to these questions should be on the top of the list.

When proponents of various theories of evolution, be they scientists, philosophers or others, speak their piece, they should be asked these three mystery questions. And only a, "I don't know" response is not intellectually acceptable.

The core principle of Scientism is that numerical quantification is required to arrive at truth. The next chapter, The Human Signaler, will accommodate that principle.

Chapter 6

THE HUMAN SIGNALER

(Caveat emptor: This chapter is a section of an open letter that I wrote to Pope Francis shortly after his election by the papal conclave. Since then, some of the biological figures quoted have changed. Also, I personally made the mathematical calculations and thought you should know that I never got above an average grade in mathematics and now, as an 82 year-old physician, I dare not try again. I raise these facts to forewarn those who are understandably interested in fact checking. But whatever the accuracy of the calculations, the key message is that all the numbers are unequivocally astronomical!)

Regarding the potential existence of a personal God, few, if any, arguments deal with the enormity of the "numbers" in the human body to support such a possibility. Arguments, instead, are based principally on the use of questionable reasoning and limited analytic tools. The principal scientific approach of this letter is based on the inexplicable mega trillions of "signaling" numbers which occur in a human and the proposed existence of the Human Signaler which directs such signals.

Signaling is a generally accepted scientific phenomenon, including by the scientific community. So we have a baseline of common belief to build upon. Signaling simply means that something happens by something making it happen. This "something" is a signal. There are four primary types of signaling activities in the human body which take place in order to create and maintain life. They are a) in the creation of cells and other body components b) within each cell c) between and among such cells and d) and by external factors which impact the aforementioned. I propose the existence of a fifth entity where a) b) c) and d) are instructed to perform and coordinate their trillions upon trillions of intended signaling functions which are necessary for life. I call this entity the Human Signaler, and its nature and location are unknown.

HUMAN BODY NUMBERS, FUNCTIONS AND SIGNALS

The technology to quantify the number of cells, the natural elements contained in them, their functions, countless interactions and what external factors impact them is in its infancy. What we do know, however, is that such numbers are beyond human comprehension. I remember well when I was in elementary school how overwhelmed I was when thinking about the number, one million. A billion, let alone a trillion, wasn't in my vocabulary, let alone in my imagination. Today, we commonly speak of trillions as an afterthought and are becoming intellectually and emotionally immune to the immensity of such numbers. Hopefully, the awareness of the *mega trillion* numbers of physical and mental signal- dependent entities in the human body which permit its existence will lessen such immunity sufficiently enough to open the door of intellectual curiosity and wonderment regarding why and how we are born, live, behave and die.

THE BRAIN

Let's begin with the most interesting of all entities in the universe— those three pounds of mysterious flesh which we call the brain. There are close to 100 billion neurons or nerve cells in the human brain. Each neuron connects with other neurons through their synapses in order to transmit messages for some type of action, be it mental or physical. According to some estimates there are at least 100 trillion synapses in the brain or 100,000,000,000, all either in action or getting ready for action at a single point in time!

The brain also has three types of glial cells— microglia, astrocytes and oligodendrocytes— which support the neurons and are estimated to be approximately three times greater in number than neurons for a total of 300 billion of them.

What is little-appreciated is that both the brain and the rest of the body are permeated and largely controlled by water and electricity. Water and electricity play an essential role in every cell and have a physical presence in the 400,000 billion neurons and glial cells combined, amounting to a total of 800,000 billion presences. All functions of the brain are dependent on them. Technology cannot measure these mega trillions of signaling-based functions. The numbers are currently beyond calculation, and it's fascinating to note that it is estimated that such numbers exceed all the trillions of stars in our galaxies which are estimated to be 3 trillion times a hundred billion, or 3 followed by 23 zeroes!

The brain also has its arteries, capillaries and veins. I could find no accurate measure of the total number of cells in these vessels. But the arteries and capillaries carry oxygen and nutrients to each brain cell which permit, like water and electricity, all cell signals to perform their duties. Carbon dioxide is then produced which also has the same numerical 400 billion presences in the cells as oxygen.

Lest we forget, we are talking about only three pounds of flesh less than the weight of a robust Easter ham.

THE TOTAL BODY INCLUDING THE BRAIN

Let's now visit the numbers in the total body, including the brain, and just consider only a few facts regarding the awe-provoking world of numbers. It's estimated there are 10 trillion cells in the total body with countless signaling-induced functions but let's consider only two— those by genes and methylation.

Though there are slightly more, making the assumption that there are 20,000 genes in each cell, we end up with a total of 200,000 trillion cellular genes controlling cell functions, way beyond technology's current capacity to quantify. But let's take an absurdly low estimate of 1,000 gene-controlled cell functions which amounts to 200,000,000 trillion signal- based functions!

Methylation consists of a simple chemical unit comprising of carbon and hydrogen which interact with numerous other molecules and changes the behavior of such molecules in either a positive or negative way. Examples of these molecules are enzymes, genetic entities such as DNA, protein, nerves and neurotransmitters. *It's estimated that the body's methylation processes occur close to one billion times per second and in just one minute, 60 billion times!*

(Here's a function that I read about and find hard to believe even though it was reported by distinguished researchers. It deals with smell. They estimate that humans can distinguish over 1 trillion scents.)

The following is an example of mind-boggling numbers, let alone unique functions, which are recently fascinating physicians and scientists. It's estimated that there 10 times as many single cell bacteria in the body than human cells which play a critical role in human health from nutrition to disease. (This type of presence in a human body can be considered a metaorganism or microbiome). Ten times 10 trillion human cells amount to 100 trillion bacteria, which weigh even more than the 3 pounds of brain flesh. It's estimated that there are 400 more microbial or bacterial genes in the body than human ones which estimates amount to 800,000 trillion. Then there are also viruses or bacteriophages which interact with these bacteria. It's estimated there are 10 bacteriophages for each bacterium which amount to 1000 trillion viruses.

So far I've been talking about numbers of cells and functions within them. But body cells also send messages to different other types of body cells which are not connected to each other through the circulatory system. For example, the immune system sends antibodies to fight bacteria and viruses at the specific point of their attack in the body. The pituitary gland sends hormones to stimulate the activation of other hormones such as those in the thyroid, adrenal and reproductive glands. The miraculous *in utero* development of a fetus requires untold numbers of signals from developing tiny toenails to the formation of the mysterious three pounds of flesh.

Then there are also cellular functions which are initiated inside but occur outside the body such as movement of all kinds from speaking to kneeling in prayer and talking to God; from constructing the Roman Coliseum to painting a portrait to playing soccer; from typing on the computer laptop to playing the piano; from dancing the tarantella to dueling to voting; from walking to running to writing a letter to a loved one and sending a Christmas gift to one's mother and father; to be fortunate enough to eat a splendid, though difficult to find, *Bollito Misto* or reading a good book both of which can elicit a variety of feelings from sadness to gladness.

(Speaking about *Bollito Misto*, about 20 years ago I had lunch with the great opera tenor, Luciano Pavarotti, at his favorite Italian restaurant *San Domenico* in Manhattan. We discovered that we both loved this dish but bemoaned the fact that we couldn't find a chef who could prepare it as they do in Emiglia Romagna, Italy).

THE MIND

Modern science is now exploring ways to locate the mind, as a distinct entity from the brain, let alone demonstrate its existence and nature. There's now a rapidly expanding specialty, experimental philosophy, where laboratory tests are employed in an attempt to locate and characterize it. It measures how people react to certain situations such as by utilizing the use of verbal responses and where the activity is located by brain imaging scans.

The mind contains within it boundless, immeasurable numbers of thoughts, feelings and other signal-induced, daily mental functions which have not been quantified. To complicate things, their definitions are not precise and oftentimes overlap. As previously stressed, words were made to communicate and not to define. For example, what is this thing called love? It wears many faces. Having said this, the following are examples of the mind's signal-induced mental activities: Consciousness or awareness of one's existence and self, recognition, recall, love of many types, hate, altruism, schadenfreude, rationalization, curiosity, sorrow, smiling, happiness, jealousy, envy, suffering, anxiety, depression, phobias, ambition, aggression, submission, domination, optimism, pessimism, friendship, loyalty, patriotism, cynicism, thinking, contemplation, reasoning in all walks of life from planning a wedding to ways to construct weapons of mass destruction, dreams, creativity, spiritualism, wisdom and, yes, faith in a personal God and life after death.

CONSCIOUSNESS

Aristotle wrote, "In everything natural, there is something marvelous" but I consider the mystery of consciousness, the act of being aware of oneself, the most provocative and mysterious of all. It's the threshold to most of life's experiences from awakening to sleep or, as we shall see, from awakening to awakening. We haven't the slightest idea of what it is, nor what kinds or how many signals cause it to happen. But there's one indisputable fact. Most of life's experiences require signals of being conscious, so the act of consciousness is inextricably bound to all such acts of life.

SLEEP—THE SUBCONSCIOUS CONSCIOUSNESS

When I was a student at Jefferson Medical College in Philadelphia, it was generally believed that the sleeping brain was a quiet organ taking a rest from the turmoil of the wakened world seeking peace. But now we know it's just the opposite and an extremely active one using trillions of signals per second and, I believe, very much conscious of itself. The activity which is most fascinating to me are dreams which are oftentimes far more exciting than the conscious life. I often wonder why there is a stream of unending stories and plots with complicated scenes which have never been or could ever be experienced. For example, I would, while vigorously flapping my arms as ersatz wings, frequently fly over cities and mountains encountering a broad variety of adventures. When I dream of old folks who have left us, they are usually young in appearance and happen in scenes that never occurred or not physically capable of happening. As in movie films, dreams require a plot and script, actors, lighting and production over a period of time. The current belief is that we dream about six times a night during which the brain creates all types of creative productions more in one night than a major Hollywood movie company can produce in a year!

There is no way to calculate the number of signals the sleeping brain employs for one second, one night or a lifetime, but, they are, "Out of sight."

EXTERNAL BODY SIGNALING

The total numbers of signaling and resulting functions which occur in a human being caused by external body factors and how they influence the internal signaling and activity are virtually unquantifiable. They are everywhere and constantly in action. To my knowledge, no one has written a sweeping description of the vastness of this external-internal signaling interconnectivity which continues during sleep.

External signaling can roughly be divided into a very broad and a more limited, epigenetic-like one. Let's start with a very small list of the former: It's what we eat, sunshine, darkness, interaction with people in innumerable situations ranging from family to the workplace, silence, noise, smell, traffic tickets, paying taxes—a powerful, disruptive psychological factor—reading, Internet, television, radio, attending a performance at La Scala of Verdi's thrilling unsurpassed opera, Otello, falling in or out of love and an inspired or uninspired Church sermon.

LIVING AS A SIGNALING FUNCTION

It occasionally triggers the wondering part of my brain when scientists speak of a cell function. They invariably relate it to a specific purpose— *and let's not forget this*! For example, mitochondria, the furnaces of the cell, have a critical purpose which is to metabolize sugar and fats to produce energy. Also, ribosomes in the cell function to produce proteins which are the messengers of the cells. But I can't recall anyone mentioning "living" as a specific cell function. The reason? There isn't a measurable specific "living" signal as such. But I consider it the most important function of all for what's the purpose of cells but to first live in order to create and maintain human life from conception to the final moment? And this living signaling process goes on in ten trillion body cells every moment of every day.

FACTORS OF TIME AND CHANGE

At this point you have probably become immune to the staggering numbers quoted, though there are mega x mega trillions more. The numbers cited, however, refer only to a single point in time. But practically everything in the human organism is in constant flux from the beginning to the end of life. The signaling is non-stop, but, for simplification, let's once more assume they occur each second. The following are six examples of the enormity of the kinds of numbers we're dealing with:

Each cell in the body has one billion ATP energy molecules. ATP causes the generation of incalculable signals, but let's assume an absurdly low number of a thousand. One billion x 1 thousand x 10 trillion body cells x 31,536,000 (seconds in a year) amounts to 315,360,000,000,000,0 00,000,000,000,000,000 signals.

There are close to 100 trillion brain synapses; multiplied by 31,536,000 annual seconds amount to 3,153,600,000,000,000,000,000 signals each year.

It was mentioned that there are 200,000,000 trillion gene signaling functions going on. Yes, some genes are dormant but it requires signaling to keep them dormant. Let's assume an average lifespan of 70 years. Gene signaling numbers x annual seconds x 70 amounts to 441,504,000,000,0 00,000,000,000,000,000 lifetime signals.

It was also mentioned that there are about one billion methylation processes going on each second brought about by signaling. One billion x annual seconds x 70 amounts to 2,207,520,000,000,000,000 signals.

Let's now consider living signals only as single ones. The 10 trillion body cells are living at a point in time. Billions of cells periodically die such as in the gastrointestinal tract and are then replaced by signaling growth factors. They are not included in these calculations but they are also numerically in the mega trillion leagues. Over a 70-year period the number of the living signals amounts to 22,075, 200, 000,000,000,000,000.

Regarding the bacterial metaorganism or microbiome, there are 800 trillion bacterial genes in the body, and though there are many more, let's assume that they have only one signaling-based function. Over a 70 year period the total signaling number is 1,766, 016, 000,000,000,000,000,000.

Now let's return to the present moment. As I am writing, I am conscious both of myself and the fact that I am writing this letter. My eyes are focused on the note pad; my brain is thinking about what to write and how to express it; my brain is also instructing my hand how to hold the pen and how to move my hand in order to write what I want to express;

my heart is beating sending oxygenated blood to my entire body; my blood pressure is being maintained to prevent me from going into shock or having a hypertensive crisis; my liver is detoxifying a pharmaceutical I took an hour ago for a neck injury; my lungs are breathing in oxygen and expelling carbon dioxide; my gastrointestinal system is digesting a morsel of toast and butter that I ingested about 15 minutes ago; I now hear the coffee pot perking and can smell the coffee's aroma; my immune system is battling ever present attacking pathogens, and my body muscles are working together to prevent me from falling off the chair; I just uncrossed my legs for an unknown reason; my toenails are slowly growing and my head hairs are in the process of inexorably leaving my scalp. All the cells in my body are performing their biochemical signaling functions that are necessary for the aforementioned activities to occur. And all, from individual cell function to body balance, require mega trillions upon mega trillions of signals to happen at each point in time.

So what does Scientism have to say about these mega trillion of signals which are all part of creating and maintaining human existence? How does it happen? What scientific method could be employed to make sense out of the dynamics of its entirety? Mathematics and the use of computers would theoretically be the appropriate tools. The problem is that classic, probability and Bayesian mathematics along with computational modeling are of little help. Ask any mathematician! For your information, I have, and they have no answer except that it is a mystery.

So what's the story? Can these mega trillions of signals be simply random events and happen by chance without a unifying force directing them to the intended purpose which is to live? Or is there such a force? The evidence certainly supports such a force which I call the Human Signaler. And, if so, what is this mysterious signaler or force and how did it come to be?

Athens versus Jerusalem

Elijah in Heaven observing philosophers Plato and Aristotle
(School of Athens by Raphael)

Chapter 7

PUTTING IT ALL TOGETHER

With fresh eyes, an attempt was made to view the evidence of the existence of a personal god by proposing a unique epistemological approach, the Emoji Brain, versus that of the standard, more limited approaches of Scientism utilizing the scientific method and the elaborate use of words commonly employed by philosophers, theologians and religious and secular intellectuals. The primary objective of this book is to encourage influential religious advocates of diverse types to employ such evidence in their educational efforts to support the potential existence of such a personal god. It's important to note that it is not intended to support any particular religion and its transcendental beliefs. Let's not forget, however, that much of the attack on the existence of God is done indirectly by attacking religion, its beliefs and rituals. For example, if God is all good, how can there be evil in the world? If he is omnipotent, can he make 2+2=5?

Before signing off, let's review a few highlights and also add some helpful thoughts to what has already been written.

There's little doubt that the belief in the Judeo-Christian personal god is on a seemingly inexorable technology-driven decline. Attempts to reverse this trend by religious advocates preaching messages such as God's love for mankind, the beauty of faith and the promise of an afterlife are not doing the job. In fact, a number of recent, highly popular and influential books on religion with favorable reviews in prestigious publications have been written by atheists and agnostics, some of whom are scientists.

There is, therefore, an urgent, immediate need for a new educational approach that is concrete, factual and sufficiently persuasive to penetrate the modern mind in order to counter the anti-God movement, and that approach is primarily through the Emoji Brain epistemological system. That's why it was essential to grasp and understand the chapter on epistemology for it's the foundation for the subsequent supportive arguments that followed.

In the final analysis, arguments, both pro and con, regarding the existence of a personal god revolve around the combination and oftentimes manipulation of three fundamental epistemological categories. They are cause, effect and purpose. What makes something happen, what is that something and for what purpose? So, let's take a hard look at how atheists, agnostics and Godists apply this threesome but first start out on something where these schools of thought agree. In the Transcendental Search discussion it's clearly demonstrated that it is natural for the human brain to search for things small to things transcendental such as a God and an afterlife. It's in our DNA, or RNA, or maybe somewhere else. But, after that, in the Science and Universe, Evolution and Human Signaler categories comes the big differences for the battle for truth. And here is where the puzzle originates.

As we will see, the concept of the existence of cause, effect and purpose is generally accepted by Godists while selectively questioned and even denied by agnostics and atheists particularly when dealing with a personal god. But this pattern of selectivity of the latter groups contradicts the way they deal with life. For example, scientists conduct their laboratory experiments to determine what purposes the things that they measure have. What is the purpose of insulin? It causes the effect of the lowering of blood sugar. What does the heart do? It causes the heart to pump blood for the effect of delivering such blood to body cells for the purpose of delivering oxygen and nutrients to body cells. Agnostic and atheistic scientists and elaborate use of words philosophers readily accept the existence of cause, effect and purpose in such laboratory studies, however, paradoxically, find it difficult to accept this triad when it comes to the existence of a God, let alone a personal one. But isn't the formation of the universe a natural laboratory experiment?

A major tenant of Scientism requires the use of numbers as part of its epistemology system. Well, the Human Signaler discussion certainly abundantly fulfils this requirement. In the discussion, it was pointed out that there are mega trillions of signals occurring each second in the human body from the zygote to one's final hour which phenomenon is far beyond any explanation offered by the scientific method, including mathematics, as well as the elaborate use of words. It's proposed that there must a single force, the human signaler, which coordinates such astronomical numbers of signals. What else? And it is an unequivocal legitimate scientific question to ask what caused the human signaler? A Universal Signaler?

In order to more precisely characterize the modern anti-god mentality, I decided to run a thought experiment encounter with a bright, intellectually honest astrophysicist-philosopher atheist to discuss three topics— The Big Bang, Evolution and the Human Signaler. I also decided that it was best to conduct it at dinner time at my home where there is no shortage of cocktail and wine supplies. Do you remember the Harvard's Law Club *In Vino Veritas?*

Sometimes I find it difficult to shed my humility but I must confess I'm not a bad cook. I prepared small-sized clams oreganato, escarole with truffle-infused olive oil and my secret recipe, pasta alla *Messicana*. I have a spectacular secret recipe for gazpacho which I modified into the pasta gravy.

Below is an abbreviated version of our delightful dinner discussion.

Halfway through the pasta I felt it was time to get down to business and asked the first question, knowing full well what his answer would be, "Duca, what caused the Big Bang?"

Without hesitation, he replied, "I don't know. Nobody knows."

"What are some of the possibilities?"

"You got me there, Steve. What preceded the Big Bang could have happened in a physical world different than what happened after and even up to today. For example, our four categories of energy, gravity, electromagnetism and weak and strong nuclear energy did not exist before and only came into being a millionth of a second or so after it happened."

"So it's a complete mystery and the scientific community is clueless—correct?"

"Correct."

We both paused and took to our wine. I then commented, "Scientifically speaking, the act of creation, making something out of nothing, certainly should be on the list of possibilities. Correct?"

Duca paused, and then somewhat reluctantly, answered, "That is correct, but highly improbable."

"Why do you say that?"

"Because it's a virtual impossibility because it defies the laws of thermodynamics."

"Duca, but you just said the laws of physics might have been different before the Big Bang. And also, it all started with the Cosmic Egg, the size of a fertilized egg or zygote which led to cosmic inflation and a vast universe that's still expanding. If that's not creation, what is?"

Duca smiled and remarked, "Steve, you're trying to corner me by implying that God could have created the universe. Correct?"

"Duca, not so. You atheists are a paranoid bunch. Every time God is mentioned or even inferred, you guys have an emotional reaction instead of an objective, scientific one. The scientific method is woefully inadequate to characterize the origin of the universe but creation is a valid theoretical possibility and you and your colleagues refuse to even address it as a scientific option."

Silence prevailed as we finished off what was remaining of our pasta. Wearing a broad smile, Duca broke the silence and asked, "Steve, what's next on your list? I'm ready."

"It's the teleological argument of Paley and the watchmaker regarding the existence of God. Practically all philosophers of all stripes, including profoundly Christian ones, reject his argument as faulty by using the elaborate epistemological use of words which methods in themselves are all faulty. Also, as you know, the scientific method is useless when dealing with the watch and watchmaker.

"Now I want you to try mightily to be objective and answer this question 'If you, yourself, stumbled upon a watch in Central Park what would immediately jump to mind? I mean immediately."

"Steve, I know about your Emoji Brain concept and, yes, my brain, like any other normal one, would inform me that someone lost it. Now you don't have to goad me into asking further questions. Yes, if I opened it and saw how intricately it was put together I would conclude that it was designed by what Paley called a watchmaker.

"Look, though not so with most philosophers, the teleological argument is the most understandable and acceptable to most people and

I would urge you to milk that cow. It's a huge door opener with the least resistance which would welcome the knock."

He paused, took to his wine and then made an interesting introspective observation. "Steve, I think you have the mistaken impression that I fit the mold of the prototype atheist—too stubborn as hell to objectively discuss God, particularly the biblical one. I believe it was Pascal of Pascal's Wager, who said that certain men fear and hate religion for it may be true."

I couldn't help but make another observation which I found common among Duca's colleagues. They find it emotionally difficult to say *I don't know!* I remember well that my medical school professor of pediatrics took it upon himself as a special crusade to teach the students, particularly those who stubbornly held on to incorrect information, to confess that they don't know.

We again separately reached for the wine and poured a healthy dose. It was evolution-discussion time.

I began with a bit of history. "Duca, I really feel sorry for you and your colleagues because you all were on a psychedelic high and relieved after Darwin's evolutionary theory was prematurely wildly and blindly embraced by the entire secular community. Finally, science had discovered that there was no need for God. Evolution explained all. It's a blind physical process of natural selection subject to random mutations and the impact of the environment. Yet, as you are well aware, there was, using the scientific method, no proof to back it up, and its recent legitimate demise is rarely announced. Epigenetics, how gene expression is altered without any change or mutation of gene structure, and the three Big Bang biological mysteries are huge factors that the scientific method cannot adequately analyze and seem to avoid perhaps because it legitimately raises the highly controversial issue of Intelligent Design that occurred in our school system a while back."

Apparently taken off guard, Duca asked, "Steve, refresh my memory. What specifically are these three big mysteries?"

"They are abiogenesis, self- organization and emerging phenomena. How does inanimate or dead matter divide and become alive; how does it then organize itself in various complicated systems from individual cells to body organs and how do these organized systems become more sophisticated going from single cell organisms to a human being as evolution proceeds? And how do they work together with the purpose—yes, Duca, they have an obvious purpose—to create and sustain life?"

Duca, with the broadest of smiles, remarks, "Now, Steve, I'm going to beat you to the punch. The scientific method has no answer or even a credible theory to explain these huge biological phenomena. Something or things are making the mystery happen. Did I get it right?"

I couldn't help but laugh and remarked, "You're doing quite well. If things keep going the way they are, you may end up a traditional agnostic, or even a Maybe-Ist one, by grappa time which seems to be here, so let's have one."

After the first sip, Duca waxed philosophic. "Steve, I appreciate what you're up to, and you're doing a superb job, and, believe it or not, though I am a stubborn, emotional atheist, I am open and listening closely because I, as a scientist, should as a professional responsibility. So keep going to the next subject of the Human Signaler and the trillions of signals, which phenomenon, may I personally add, impresses me above the others yet, strangely enough, like the three mysteries is hardly seriously discussed in scientific and philosophical circles. Where in God's name are your influential religious leaders?"

That's the sixty-four thousand dollar question, and I decided to let it drop in order to stay focused on the subject of our conversation.

"Duca, I'm happy to hear you're on board so I'll make it quick. There are trillions of signals going on each second in the human body; I'll repeat, each second, with trillions of causes, effects and molecular, biochemical and biological purposes with the primary purposes of creating and sustaining life let alone from growing toenails to experiencing consciousness. Neither the scientific method, including mathematics and computer modeling, can begin to touch the surface of how these things occur each second during a lifetime but the Emoji Brain, with its accrued and assimilated knowledge and wisdom easily grasps the more than obvious fact that they must be coordinated by something—and this something I call the Human Signaler. And it doesn't take a genius to conclude that this Human Signaler must have been caused from something and that something might be a Universal Signaler with an intelligence to guide the entire process. And, how about this: It's possible that this something could be the same entity that's behind the Big Bang and evolution because, after all, they are both part of a continuum."

We gulped down the remaining grappa, and I decided it was time to wrap up our conversation with a summary.

"Duca, let me summarize our discussion and make sure I got it right. Also, I'd appreciate any additional thoughts or suggestions that you might have."

Surprisingly, before I could begin, Duca called me to a halt. "Steve, no need. I got the story. From my point of view, which would be similar to most influential atheists and agnostics, your overall epistemological concept of the Emoji Brain, the Big Bang, evolution and the Human Signaler is not only worthy of respect but extremely challenging. But let me warn you that it will create an energetic backlash of an anti-Emoji Brain school of secular intellectuals. For, remember, as you constantly preach, all systems are faulty. And who knows how those you call the Godists or religious groups will react. They may miss the point that you're trying to make. You're not specifically advocating the existence of the biblical God which they would understandably welcome but just some type of vague personal god who exists somehow and somewhere. On the other hand, there are lots of exceptional ones that will probably catch on and carry the ball.

"Now there's the rest of the population who are in the vast majority and care less about philosophy and all the other high-level intellectual tools of analysis. And, without any doubt, having some respectable and effective communication leaders, be they agnostics, atheists or Godists, publicly support your concept will help penetrate these barriers. Also, you must make clear, particularly to Christian leaders, that your fundamental objective deals with the fading existence of God in all religions and your message applies to all of them."

Duca paused and asked, "Steve, let's have a half-glass of grappa."

I poured, we sipped it, and he continued. "Cutting through all the barriers to a successful launch of your book, there is one key and fundamental objective. It's making clear that the epistemological foundation of your Emoji Brain concept versus the scientific method and elaborate wordy philosophical arguments does a far superior job of grasping reality and the possibility or probability of the existence of God. And let me tell you it won't be easy to do. Who cares about epistemology!"

He paused, we finished off our grappas and he concluded: "I agree with you in that what is needed is a core group of energetic, creative religious leaders to package and simplify your message into their styles of communication in order to effectively deliver it to their constituents. And, by the way, I believe our country is where the action is. Start here and then follow the bouncing ball."

I must confess I was impressed by Duca's astute reading of how to move forward. But I wondered about something else. The man understood my concept and I wondered whether it had any impact on his atheism. I then asked, "Duca, Are you ready to become an agnostic or even a Maybe-Ist one?"

Duca smiled and warmly replied, "Not yet, my friend. Not yet. But give me time."

There's another revealing phenomenon not mentioned in the previous pages where, though rarely mentioned, on which secular intellects and Godists epistemologically agree. It deals with what I call Seven Billionism which is a form of a collective world Emoji Brain. There are a little more than seven billion earth's inhabitants with many different cultures and genetic backgrounds. Yet despite this broad world-wide diversity there are core commonalities. Seven Billionism proposes that truth can best be known by how an individual reacts to the entire act of living which capacity, in various degrees, is commonly shared by all of earth's inhabitants. It involves observation, experience, analysis, judgment and action, among other human qualities. It embraces the total human experience and accrued wisdom which, needless to say, is vastly broader than the scope of Scientism and elaborate, wordy philosophy.

Let's assume that all of earth's inhabitants are well educated and asked to read the following blurb about apples published in an international prestigious journal:

"Many know about the Biblical story of the tempting apple, Adam and Eve, the only people who never had in-laws or belly buttons, and the serpent, and how a few bites taken by a man and woman created universal human suffering including the need to have a job and work for a living. Way back in history, however, the apple became a symbol of love and beauty. There are currently over 7,000 varieties of them with different colors and consistencies to touch and taste. There are songs about apples and, in common parlance, bad folks who are sometimes called 'bad apples.' There is apple butter and apple pie. There are thousands of apple orchards to behold and more than one Newtonian one to observe. And finally there is the biggest one of all, The Big Apple otherwise known as New York City."

The world's seven billion Emoji Brains, based on trillions of past accumulated icon and symbol experiences, can, after reading this paragraph, easily and quickly comprehend and accept the truth contained in it, let alone wonder about and come up with new ideas and thoughts about the entire global apple scenario. Now imagine how the use of the scientific method could take us to the same level of comprehension. Imagine how much research and how many laboratory experiments would be necessary. For example, one would have to visit all the apple orchards in the world simply in order to count how many there are and then photograph apple samples from each one to determine the physical characteristics of each type. Then have multiple apple-tasting groups around the world for each of the 7,000 varieties in order to determine whether there are differences in tastes of the apples themselves as well as in their uses in pastries and other food forms. This project alone—and there are obviously others— would take billions of dollars and many decades to accomplish but would never be done for no one would ever sponsor it let alone conclude that it is necessary!

Regarding the application of the epistemological elaborate use of words to the apple scenario, we will encounter the identical dilemma as with the scientific method. It would, however, first require the facts and conclusions generated by the scientific research conducted on which to base its facts and elaborations thereafter. It simply cannot be done.

Given the circumstances of the apple presentation, secular intellectuals would, along with the seven billion others, readily accept its contents. After all, they read thousands of stories about all kinds of subject matter and reports in multiple journals and newspapers as well as view television and cyberspace and have no problem accepting their contents. But somehow when it comes to God they demand more and apply the scientific method and elaborate use of words which do not do well on the Emoji Brain Scorecard.

Many have asked me why atheists are so passionate about eliminating the belief in a personal god. I don't know. Aristotle defined man as a rational creature while DeFelice defines man as a creature that rationalizes— for whatever reason.

Getting to the subject of the transcendental search previously addressed, an identical epistemological dilemma stubbornly persists. Within the brains of earth's seven billion inhabitants there are trillions of transcendental thoughts, feelings and strongly held beliefs a substantial number dealing with transcendental entities including a personal god and life after death. In one way or another such beliefs are naturally in the brain of peoples of all cultures. To identify, quantify and objectively analyze such beliefs would require the scientific method before the wordy elaborators could render their subjective opinions. Without the results of such studies there is hardly any semblance of objectivity.

Regarding Seven Billionism the compelling conclusion is that in countless walks of life the Emoji Brain comprehends vastly more than the scientific method and elaborate wordy attempts in dealing with the reality of life, including a personal god.

To religious leaders I would urge you to think about and expand the apple scenario or similar examples and analogies according to your audience, for it is easy to understand and opens many doors to additional creative thought.

In conclusion, the weight of evidence, scientific and otherwise, perceived by the Emoji Brain, heavily supports the existence of Maybe-Ism, some type of directional, yes, intelligent force or personal god which is involved in the formation of the Universe and evolution. Though it does intellectually take us to the existence of such an entity, it does not take us to a personal relationship between an individual and this entity and the belief in an afterlife. This requires the thing called faith which is not the subject of this book but, however, I'd like to offer some observations and thoughts before signing off.

First of all, what is faith? If one conducts a cyberspace search for a definition, one will enter another epistemological quagmire and emerge unenlightened, if not confused. Its roots are derived from the Greek word *pistis* which means "to be persuaded" and which is the necessary step in order to begin to pursue it. If you recall my personal experience with faith, the first step was to be intellectually convinced of the existence of a personal god but, even after becoming convinced I did not experience faith; I had to be persuaded. I did this by the tenacious exercise of my will and persuading myself by praying and talking to God on a daily basis and hanging in there and somehow along the way faith arrived. I am reminded of the story of Thomas Aquinas's sister when she asked him, "Thomas, I want to be a saint. How do I do this?" He succinctly replied, "My dear sister, you must *will it.*"

Both public and private surveys and studies in the United States consistently reveal two growing cultural dynamics. Though the depth of belief in a personal god is diminishing a substantial majority of men and women, including scientists, continue to hold on to the belief of such an existence or that of an ersatz god such as spiritualism. The second finding is an exploding degree of modern technology- driven insecurity even among the wealthy. Heidegger wrote of angst or existential anxiety, that the simple act of existing itself is a state of anxiety. St. Augustine, long before, proclaimed on the first page of his Confessions that we are anxious until we find rest in the biblical God. Imagine the degree of it today in our unsettling age of disruptive technology.

This duality, the persistent belief in a personal god and exploding insecurity certainly reflects a widespread cultural receptivity of a solid and persuasive argument for the existence of such a God. This book hopefully offers such an argument as the necessary first step before attempts at persuading men and women to "will" themselves to seek the faith. Regarding the latter, this can best be done by multiple efforts of influential religious advocates to encourage men and women to tenaciously bite the bullet and embark on this transcendental voyage to closely encounter a personal god.

One other encouraging point to religious advocate leaders: You have a fearless and highly influential member on your team in the person of the theologian giant, St. Thomas Aquinas. One of his major messages was that faith and reason, which includes science, are compatible and should boldly be employed as a team when seeking the truth. After all, the truth is the truth—no matter from whence it comes!

The Scholastic Catholic Theological Principle, *Credo ut intelligam, intelligo ut credam* or *I believe in order to understand, and I understand in order to believe* was his guiding light. And it should be yours.

About the Author

As a young medical doctor, Dr. DeFelice became interested in why with all our technology we have few cures. And about the same time, while stationed at WRAIR, the Walter Reed Army Institute of Research as Chief of Pharmacology, during the Vietnam War, he became equally concerned with the dramatic social changes that began then and which alarmed him. Regarding actual cures he personally brought the naturally occurring substance, carnitine, into the United States, conducted the first clinical trials on it and managed through a fascinating journey to obtain FDA approval for its life-saving treatment for the fatal disease in children, Primary Carnitine Deficiency. He was also responsible for launching lithium for the treatment of manic-depression or bipolar disease.

In 1976 he founded and is Chairman of FIM, the Foundation for Innovation in Medicine whose mission is to increase medical discovery.

His personal experience with God began when he was in college and during medical school, both secular institutions. He became interested in Catholicism and attended night and summer classes at Villanova and St. Joseph's universities where he learned not only about Christianity but other world religions. At about the same time our destabilizing social revolution had suddenly begun and traditional institutions such as the family and other Judeo-Christian traditions came under attack. He observed that a major driving force was the subtle, but powerful beginning of the anti-God atheistic movement which has now infiltrated major segments of our culture. He wrote this book to counter the faulty arguments supporting atheism—and they are all faulty.